SOCIAL CHANGE AND STRATIFICATION IN POSTWAR CZECHOSLOVAKIA

Social Change and Stratification in Postwar Czechoslovakia

JAROSLAV KREJČÍ
University of Lancaster

Columbia University Press
New York
1972

Published in Great Britain in 1972 by The Macmillan Press Ltd

Copyright © 1972 Jaroslav Krejčí

Printed in Great Britain

Library of Congress Cataloging in Publication Data

Krejčí, Jaroslav, 1916–
    Social change and stratification in postwar
Czechoslovakia

    1.   Czechoslovak Republic—Social conditions.
1.   Title
HN418.C9K68   309.1′437′04   72–80480
ISBN 0–231–03685–X

To my wife

Publishers' Note

The series of eleven volumes entitled 'Political and Social Processes in Eastern Europe' is the result of a British inter-university, inter-disciplinary comparative study, sponsored by the Social Science Research Council. Professor Ghiţa Ionescu was the organiser and co-ordinator of the research work (1968–71).
The volumes are as follows:

Ghiţa Ionescu (University of Manchester): The Evolution of the Socialist State

Jane Cave (University of Birmingham), R. Amann (University of Birmingham), L. Blit (University of London), R. W. Davies (University of Birmingham), T. Podolski (Portsmouth Polytechnic), and G. Sakwa (University of Bristol): Politics and the Polish Economy

David Lane (University of Essex) and George Kolankiewicz (University of Swansea) (*editors*): Social Groups in Polish Society

Jaroslav Krejčí (University of Lancaster): Social Change and Stratification in Postwar Czechoslovakia

Vladimir V. Kusin (University of Glasgow): Political Grouping in the Czechoslovak Reform Movement

A. H. Brown (University of Oxford) and G. Wightman (University of Glasgow): The Communist Party of Czechoslovakia

J. F. N. Bradley (University of Manchester): Czechoslovak Politics 1948–68

Phyllis Auty (University of London): The Changing Role of the Yugoslav Communist Party

R. K. Kindersley (University of Oxford): The Yugoslav Federal Assembly: Relations between Executive and Legislature

F. Singleton (University of Bradford): The Yugoslav Social Groups and Institutions

D. Matko (University of Glasgow) and D. J. R. Scott (University of Glasgow): Career Patterns of Yugoslav Decision-Makers

The individual volumes have different titles and each of them is a self-contained, independent study on a separate subject.

Together they form a tripartite analysis of three given Socialist states of Eastern Europe: Czechoslovakia, Poland and Yugoslavia, as follows:

Subject of study	Poland	Czechoslovakia	Yugoslavia
The changing role of representative institutions	Jane Cave G. Sakwa	J. F. N. Bradley	R. K. Kindersley
The changing role of the Party	Jane Cave	A. H. Brown and G. Wightman	Phyllis Auty
The changing role of the groups in the interplay between the government and the economy	L. Blit, R. W. Davies, R. Amann, and T. Podolski David Lane and George Kolankiewicz	Jaroslav Krejčí Vladimir V. Kusin	F. Singleton D. Matko and D. J. R. Scott

See for a complete description of the project in the Appendix of _The Evolution of the Socialist State_, by Ghiţa Ionescu in this series.

Each book in the series will carry its own index of names and subjects. When all eleven volumes have been published a complete synoptical index to the series will be published.

Contents

List of Tables

Preface

This book is one of a series by different authors, a part of a broader research project. The whole research, led by Professor Ghiţa Ionescu and sponsored by the S.S.R.C., deals with institutions and political processes, with the development and roles of groups in the interplay between Government, economy and political culture in three Communist countries: Czechoslovakia, Poland and Yugoslavia.

This study falls into that part of the whole project which deals with Czechoslovakia. Its subject is the concrete features of social change, especially those which are relevant to the evaluation of changes in socio-economic formations (systems) in general and those which characterise the main structural changes within Czechoslovak society in particular. This implies a short review of shifts in ethnic structure and in the relative position of the Czech and Slovak part of the state.

The main attention however is given to social stratification understood in the broad sense of groupings according to the socio-economic and power status. The development of the socio-economic groups is followed with regard to their magnitudes, positions and roles against the changing institutional background. An attempt is undertaken to discover whether the new stratification pattern has produced a cleavage which might be qualified as social classes and what is the position and structure of the new power élite.

In connection with the changes in social structure the basic relevant aspects of plan-market dichotomy are reviewed and the impact of the economic restructuring assessed. Changes in the distribution of individual incomes are juxtaposed with the shifts in the national income as a whole. The latter are especially scrutinised in view of the rate of surplus value and its use.

Further books within the project series will deal with other aspects of Czechoslovak development. The author has to refer especially to two of them: *Political Grouping in the Czechoslovak Reform Movement*, by Vladimir V. Kusin, and *The Communist Party of Czechoslovakia* by A. H. Brown and G. Wightman, which are to be published in 1972 and 1973 respectively.

Within this context, this particular book may be envisaged, to borrow Professor Ionescu's description, as the background study for better understanding of more recent events. It should however be stressed that the whole background could not be covered by it. Cultural and political development are touched only occasionally; economic issues, which are discussed more explicitly, are dealt with in view of their social implications rather than because of their own merits. By combining a sociological with a macro-economic analysis, however, an attempt is undertaken to obtain a more comprehensive and better founded picture than the use of only one method could have provided.

Acknowledgements

The author is happy to express his acknowledgements: to the S.S.R.C., sponsor of the whole project, to the Graduate Institute of International Studies in Geneva, which within the framework of a research fellowship gave him the opportunity to profit from the international libraries sited in that city, and especially to the University of Lancaster, which enabled him to undertake and complete his study and provided him with all technical facilities necessary to this end. The author is also much indebted to the University Library in general and to that of the Comenius Collection in particular. He has a special thanks to offer to Mr G. P. M. Walker, who in addition to his co-operation as librarian has undertaken the reading of the whole manuscript to improve the author's English wherever this seemed to him to be too much at loggerheads with tolerable usage. Last but not least, the author is obliged to his wife, who despite her own professional obligations has helped him to complete his study on schedule.

Abbreviations and Symbols

CS   Czechoslovakia, Czechoslovak
Kčs   Czechoslovak Crown
KSČ   Communist Party of Czechoslovakia
.   Data unknown (in tables)
—   Nil or negligible quantity, or non-existing category (in tables)

CHAPTER ONE

Main Features of the Postwar Social Change

(A) GENERAL INTRODUCTORY NOTE

Against the background of a series of comparative studies involving also Poland and Yugoslavia, an introductory note has to be said about the main specific features of Czechoslovak society and its postwar development.

Czechoslovakia is for several reasons the most suitable case of social change on Marxist lines. It is, with East Germany, the only country which in general had attained a fair degree of industrialisation and ensuing economic development, before socialisation in the Marxist–Leninist sense took place. It was, therefore, theoretically better fitted to the socialist mode of production than most other countries which now belong to the Communist orbit, including Soviet Russia.

In other respects as well, Czechoslovakia was better conditioned to the socialist transformation than any other country, including East Germany, with its high level of economic maturity. Czechs and Slovaks were nations with practically no aristocracy and with intellectuals and middle-class of, until recently, mostly peasant origin. The Czechs themselves had a peasantry participating more deeply than usual in a national culture above the folklore level, and a numerous working class, not only literate but also largely educated in a particular blend of socialist ideas and national tradition, with such highlights of reform, revolution and popular movements as Hussitism and The National Revival.

However, even under these seemingly favourable conditions, the socialist transformation of society did not take place mainly as a result of internal development. It was brought about by a particular combination of factors, among which the pre-disposition already mentioned played only a subsidiary role. Neither can the traditional Slavophile, pro-Russian feelings (revived under the combined impact of Munich, of German occupation and anti-Soviet propaganda), and of Soviet endurance and later military achievements during the war, supply a satisfactory explanation for subsequent development.

As the comparison with other Communist states of Eastern Europe reveals, neither the low degree of economic maturity nor the lack of socialist consciousness, or the existence of anti- rather than pro-Russian feelings could alter or substantially influence the common course of events brought about by a combination of internal and external pressures in the countries which, according to the Soviet-American division of the world, have fallen into the Soviet orbit.

Although the stage of economic maturity and pro- or anti-Russian feelings were virtually irrelevant for the building of socialism in a Leninist sense, they were nevertheless important, in combination with other socio-cultural factors, for the detailed shaping and adaptation of the common pattern to the particular country for its subsequent development.

The degree of industrialisation and psychological predisposition were very important factors which, in Czechoslovakia, contributed substantially to the pattern of socialist society. They enabled a large-scale homogenisation of Czech and Slovak society, starting in the wake of the war, at the very beginning of what may be called 'systemic transformation'.

The homogenisation of Czechoslovak society consisted in the reduction of several important differentials in its structure, bringing about a substantial simplification of its stratification pattern. This did not concern, as a result of large-scale nationalisation, the class differences in the strict Marxist sense only, but also, independently of it, the distribution of income and consumers' property and the living standards connected with them and (no less important through the transfer of Germans and some other minor changes) the ethnic structure, the tensions within which were the main cause for the break down of the first – in Communist terminology, bourgeois – republic. For a short period there was also a tendency towards abolition of inequalities in landed property, but it was soon commuted into the drive for collectivisation which eventually resulted in equalisation of many aspects of socio-economic life in the countryside.

On the other hand, the abolition of competing political parties performed by the Communist take-over in 1948 produced only apparent superficial unification without bringing about a corresponding homogenisation on the ideological plane. The abolition of legal opposition and concentration of political, economic and ideological authority in a highly centralised institution had a polarising rather than equalising effect on the power structure. Thus, a new kind of differentiation was produced, the impact of which countered in a way the equalisation achieved in other fields.

The magnitude of the achieved homogenisation can be documented in several ways. However, its importance may be still better assessed by looking at those aspects which happened not to be homogenised and which eventually, in confrontation with the newly established pattern of power structure, became the main reason for new tensions evoking the need for further changes. Such were mainly the differences in the level and content of education and knowledge, both outside and within the ruling party, and the ethnic differences between Czechs and Slovaks and their respective countries.

Whereas the first difference, aggravated by the continuous tension between the official and non-official interpretation of past and present facts and events, could become a visible issue only occasionally, revealing its magnitude only in the late sixties, the difference between Czechs and Slovaks, with their highly developed national consciousness accentuated by their different levels of economic and cultural development, constituted a problem which in view of the Communist concept of nationalities could hardly be denied or concealed.

It is no wonder that the thousand years during which the Slavs in Upper Hungary were politically separated from the Slavs in Bohemia and Moravia left a deep impact on the national consciousness of both peoples. The unification in 1918 occurred under conditions of inequality between Czechs and Slovaks: inequality in numbers, economic strength and cultural level. Although the Czechs, who naturally acquired a leading role, substantially helped towards the cultural emancipation of the Slovaks from the heritage of Hungarian dominance, they did not satisfy the growing needs of their weaker partner longing for a greater share of the decision making in the common state.

Paradoxically, it was the Nazi occupation of Bohemia and Moravia which enabled the Slovaks to attain a state of their own, but in the awkward position of a German satellite which in addition to its dependence was deprived of some border territory, claimed for ethnic reasons by neighbouring Hungary.

The Slovak resistance movement against the pro-Nazi régime paved the way for the reconstitution of the common state – the Czechoslovak Republic, which however, in the aftermath of the war, was conceived as a dualistic rather than unitary state. The official prewar concept of one Czechoslovak nation with two languages (Czech and Slovak) was abolished and replaced by the concept of two nationalities.[1]

With a continuing homogenisation in other aspects of Czechoslovak society it was supposed that the Czech–Slovak relationship would be gradually eased, especially as a result of bringing Slovakia to a similar economic level and standard of living to that of Czech part of the State. However, the gap was too large to be overcome in a short period, and even considering the considerable progress achieved the development in both Czech and Slovak parts of the State showed clearly the ultimate goals attainable by economic means alone were limited.

The new constitution of 1960 removed Slovakia's autonomy to a large extent. This disguised attempt to revive a more unitary state provoked widespread dissatisfaction among Slovaks, this time including large sections of the established power élite.

---

[1] The word nationality is here used in the sense in which it is understood in the whole of Europe to the East of the Rhine; that is, in its ethnic and not political sense as is the English, French and American custom. In all countries which were parts of the Romanov, Hohenzollern, Habsburg and Ottoman Empires, the nation (nationality) is a different concept from the state (statehood). The root of most political struggles during the nineteenth and the first half of the twentieth centuries lay in the claim of every nation to be provided with its own state, which might possibly include all the members of the ethnic community concerned.

Simultaneously, the homogenity of the Communist power élite in general, and in the Czech part of the State in particular, was relaxing. The continued impact of growing empirical and theoretical knowledge, especially with respect to factual development in the East and West, of natural longing for personal and national self-determination in line with national, democratic and genuinely socialist tradition, produced a general mood of unease. Utterances of misgivings appeared first among intellectuals but gradually came to be shared for different reasons by further strata of the population. All this produced a crisis which, because of the juxtaposition of two cross-cutting inter-élite differences (political and ethnic), outgrew the latent stage and took on the form of an overt and complex struggle.

The pressure for economic reform was one of the aspects, or rather outcomes, of this crisis. It originated in the growing realisation of the gap between potentialities and actual achievements, in the tension between the desire for more spontaneous creative participation in the shaping of economic life on one side, and on the other the mechanical application of blueprints, the practical fulfilment of which often contradicted economic efficiency and consequently could not satisfy the developing size and pattern of demand.

(B) ETHNIC CHANGES

With respect to the key role of the ethnic heterogeneity in the dissolution of Czechoslovakia in 1938 and 1939, and, in a way, also in the development in the late sixties, we shall turn first to the review of the changes in the ethnic structure.

In this respect Czechoslovakia underwent the greatest change during and immediately after World War II. In 1948 Czechoslovakia was ethnically more homogeneous than in 1938, when, because of ethnic tensions, she broke apart. Chronologically the main changes occurred as follows.

As a result of the Nazi racial policy, supported to a certain extent by the satellite régimes in Slovakia and Hungary, the Jewish minority virtually disappeared. In 1930 there were 357,000 persons of Jewish religion in Czechoslovakia. Of this number 205,000, mostly in Sub-Carpathian Russia (Ruthenia) and Slovakia, declared themselves, in that year, as of Jewish nationality.[1] In 1966 the number of Jews was estimated at 15,000.[2]

On 29 June 1945 Czechoslovakia agreed to cede Sub-Carpathian Russia (since then Trans-Carpathian Ukraine) to the Soviet Union. This area had according to the last prewar census (in 1930) 725,000 inhabitants of which 62·2 per cent were Russians or Ukrainians, 15·9 per cent Hungarians and 13·1 per cent of Jewish nationality.[3]

A month later the U.S.S.R., U.S.A. and U.K., at the Potsdam Conference, consented to the transfer of Germans from Czechoslovakia. This action was started at the beginning of 1946 and was concluded towards the end of that year. As a result of this transfer the number of Germans in Czechoslovakia dropped from 3,207,000 in 1930 to 165,000 in 1950 (years of censuses) or from 22·3 per cent to 1·3 per cent of population.[4]

The attempt to exchange Slovaks settled in Hungary for Hungarians from Slovakia was only partially successful. Hungarian official statistics from 1941 gave 76,000 Slovaks in which is now Hungary; according to Slovak claims however this figure is highly underrated. During the exchange negotiations 95,000 persons were listed for resettlement; however, only 73,000 actually returned to Slovakia. The number of Hungarians who left Slovakia was approximately the same.[5]

To resettle the previously German-populated territory, a reimmigration campaign was launched in 1945 to repatriate Czechs and Slovaks scattered over various countries. This campaign brought, in addition to the 73,000 Slovaks from Hungary, 121,000 reimmigrants, of which almost 40,000 were from Soviet Russia[6] to Czechoslovakia.

All these changes of course did not only homogenise the

---

[1] Unless otherwise stated, all figures are taken from the Czechoslovak Statistical Yearbooks.

[2] *The Statesman's Year-Book, 1970/71. The Atlas of Israel* (Jerusalem–Amsterdam, 1970) gives the figure at 18,000.

[3] It is not possible to assess how many of the 103,000 Jews of that area survived in or returned after the war to what is now Trans-Carpathian Ukraine.

[4] For the history and detailed balance sheet of these events see Radomír Luža, *The Transfer of the Sudeten Germans* (London, 1964).

[5] Juraj Zvara, *Maďarská menšina na Slovensku* (Bratislava, 1969) p. 64.

[6] *Czechoslovakia's New Labour Policy* (Prague, 1949) p. 27.

language structure of the country; they have simultaneously eliminated some important political tensions. To appreciate the importance of this we have to compare the shifts in the ethnic structure with the separatist or autonomist aspirations within the individual nationalities (loyalty ratio), as shown in the last prewar election results, in 1935 (see Table 1). These were the last free elections, where no political party was excluded from the contest.

Although the Communist Party at that time largely supported the extension of national minorities' rights, the Communist vote cannot be envisaged as another indicator in the context mentioned. Since the ascent of Hitler to power in Germany in January 1933, the Communist attitude to the Czechoslovak Republic became rather ambivalent. On one side the Republic as a 'bourgeois' state should be combated, on the other hand as (after the Dollfuss *coup d'état* in Austria) the only liberal democratic state in Central Europe allowing a legal existence to the Communist Party, and eventually from 1935 an ally of the Soviet Union, it should be defended. With regard to this, the Communist vote should be regarded as indicative of socioeconomic tensions rather than an indication of loyalty.

Unfortunately, as the Communist Party of Czechoslovakia cut across ethnic boundaries, its percentage of votes cannot be assessed for separate nationalities, but for individual lands only. Nevertheless, this division is also revealing. Whereas in the Czech Lands the Communist vote was less than 9 per cent, in Slovakia it attained 13 per cent and in Sub-Carpathian Russia 25·6 per cent of the poll in 1935. The socialist reformist parties (Czechoslovak and German Social Democratic parties and Czechoslovak National Socialist Party) scored 28 per cent in the Czech Lands, 14·6 per cent in Slovakia and 13·6 per cent of valid votes in Sub-Carpathian Russia.

The figures in Table 1 indicate that of the non-Czechs, who together made up almost one half of the population in Czechoslovakia in 1930, the Jews were in 1935 the only fully loyal ethnic community. Of the other nationalities, the least affected by nationalistic centrifugal aspirations were the Ruthenians. Both minorities, however, virtually disappeared, for different reasons, from the ethnic map of Czechoslovakia in 1950.[1]

---

[1] Even the number of Ruthenians (now Ukrainians), who after the cession

Table I

ETHNIC STRUCTURE AND LOYALTY RATIO IN PREWAR CZECHOSLOVAKIA

	Czechs	Slovaks	Germans	Hungarians	Russians and Ukrainians	Jews	Poles	Others	Total
Nationalities in 1930 (in per cent of resident citizens)	51·1	15·8	22·3	4·8	3·8	1·3	0·6	0·3	100·0
Votes for separatist or autonomist parties in 1935 — in per cent of the total vote	—	6·0	15·2	3·5	0·6	—	0·3	—	25·6
— in per cent of the respective nationality	—	38·0	68·2	72·9	15·8	—	50·0	—	25·6
Nationalities in 1950 (in per cent of residents)	67·9	26·3	1·3	3·0	0·6	—	0·6	0·3	100·0

Compiled from Czechoslovak *Statistical Yearbooks*. The figures for Czechs and Slovaks (who in prewar Czechoslovakia were not counted separately) are taken, for 1930, from V. Srb, 'Obyvatelstvo Ceskoslovenska v letech 1918–1968', in *Demografie* (1968) p. 302.

The election data represent the percentage of the valid votes to the Lower House of Parliament (Chamber of Deputies) given to the following parties: The Autonomist Bloc, composed mainly of the Slovak People's (Catholic) Party and three other minor parties: Slovak Nationalist Party, (Ruthenian) Autonomist Agrarian Union and Polish United Party (in East Silesia,); Sudeto-German and Carpatho-German Parties; Hungarian Christian Socialist and Nationalist Parties.

The Germans, who by their sheer numbers and the high percentage of disloyalty (which, as may be inferred from the subsequent events, increased further after 1935) represented the greatest centrifugal force within the state, similarly disappeared.[1]

The Hungarian minority, whose disloyalty ratio in 1935 was, according to our indicator, the highest among the ethnic minorities in Czechoslovakia, was considered in the aftermath of war as a hostile element. Several actions to reduce their numbers were envisaged.[2] However, after 1948, when the Communist leadership did not need to compromise as much with nationalistic feelings and also in Hungary the Communist Party became an unrivalled leading force, the oppression

---

of Ruthenia proper to Soviet Russia remained in the north-eastern fringe of Slovakia, declined considerably: from 91,000 in 1930 to 48,000 in 1950 and 35,000 in 1961. This may have resulted from the Slovak cultural influence, which in a rural population speaking an in-between dialect could enjoy a stronger institutional and prestige backing, and from the fear of that population of Soviet interference; this became unpopular especially through the attempt to bring the Greek Catholics in Slovakia (virtually all Ruthenians there belonged to this rite) over to the Orthodox rite and Muscovite jurisdiction. This issue is also mentioned on p. 36 and discussed in more detail in Vladimir V. Kusin, *Political Grouping in the Czechoslovak Reform Movement.*

[1] Further decline of the German minority – shown in Table 2 – was due partly to emigration (made possible after the tension had subsided) and partly to assimilation. The German minority became geographically too dispersed, and apparently also morally weakened, to withstand the natural pressure of environment.

[2] In addition to the exchange of population with Hungary, two actions were devised: (*a*) re-Slovakisation of those Hungarians who were supposed to be of Slovak origin, (*b*) transfer of ethnic (true) Hungarians, who did not intend to leave for Hungary, to the Czech borderland formerly settled by Germans. In the first action 327,000 persons were declared to be Slovaks. In the second action about 44,000 persons were settled in the Czech borderland, most of them forcibly. Thus it happened that the number of 'ethnic' Hungarians in Slovakia was supposed to be reduced, in 1948, to 190,000 (Zvara, *Maď'arská menšina*, pp. 66–7). In June 1948 the exchange of population with Hungary was stopped. After 1 May 1948 Hungarians who had been forcibly settled in the Czech borderlands were allowed to return. 24,000 took this opportunity. (Zvara, *Maď'arská menšina*, p. 81). The re-Slovakisation became obsolete and everybody was allowed to decide his nationality for himself. Thus it happened that the number of Hungarians in Czechoslovakia increased to 368,000 in 1950 and further to 534,000 in 1961. (In 1930 their number on the present territory was 583,000.)

measures were gradually abolished. Hungarian minority re-emerged as an important factor of heterogeneity in Slovakia.

The Polish minority underwent practically no change. Being limited to a small although economically vital area to the east of Ostrava, it represents only a local problem.

In view of the considerably reduced share of ethnic minorities in Czechoslovakia, the Czech–Slovak dualism became the salient feature of ethnic heterogeneity within the State. This is the more important because these nations live in clearly delimited territories with a different history, a different level of economic development and a different socio-cultural tinge. We shall deal with some tangible aspects of this differentiation in a separate sub-chapter (1 D).

On the other hand, a new marginal but nevertheless painful ethnic problem arose (or rather emerged from a latent to an acute stage), namely, the problem of gypsies. Growing faster in numbers than other nationalities and enjoying more possibilities not only of horizontal but also of vertical social mobility than before the war, they started to claim consideration as a separate nationality with rights guaranteed to other national minorities by the Constitutional law from 27 October 1968.[1]

In general it should be noted that the ethnic homogenisation was more thorough-going in the Czech Lands than in Slovakia. This comparative development is shown in Table 2. Also the proportion of gipsies who are not counted by the censuses underlines this difference. In 1968 it was 0·6 per cent in the Czech Lands and 3·7 per cent in Slovakia.

---

[1] Gipsies (although speaking their own language) are still officially looked upon as a socio-economic anomaly rather than an ethnic group. They are not counted by censuses, but registered by local government authorities (in 1947 101,000, of which 84,000 in Slovakia; in 1966, 222,000, of which 165,000 in Slovakia). However, these figures do not include around 50,000 of them who are supposed to be adequately integrated with the environment. Some of them have attained higher education and a good standard of living. From this group the claim for acknowledgement of gipsies as a separate nationality has been raised. Data from Vladimír Srb and Olga Vomáčková, 'Cikáni v Československu v roce 1968', in *Demografie*, XI (1969) pp. 221–9.

Table 2

ETHNIC STRUCTURE OF THE CZECH LANDS AND SLOVAKIA
(IN PER CENT OF TOTALS IN THE RESPECTIVE YEARS)

	Czech Lands				Slovakia			
	1930	1950	1961	1970	1930	1950	1961	1970
Czechs	68·4	93·8	94·3	94·7	3·6	1·2	1·1	1·1
Slovaks	0·4	2·9	2·9	3·2	67·6	86·6	85·3	85·5
Ukrainians and Russians	0·2	0·2	0·2	0·1	2·9	1·4	0·9	0·9
Poles	0·9	0·8	0·7	0·7	0·2	0·1	0·0	0·0
Germans	29·5	1·8	1·4	0·8	4·7	0·1	0·1	0·1
Hungarians	0·1	0·2	0·1	0·2	17·6	10·3	12·4	12·2
Other and not stated	0·5	0·3	0·4	0·3	3·4*	0·3	0·2	0·2

* Mainly Jews.

Sources: CS *Statistical Yearbooks*, 1957 and 1971.

(c) SOCIO-ECONOMIC CHANGES

Unlike the changes in the ethnic structure which resulted from World War II and were basically complete two years after the end of hostilities, the changes in the socio-economic structure were performed gradually and the whole process covered about fifteen years. Their primary aim was the socialisation of the means of production. The secondary aim, sometimes achieved by independent measures, was the levelling of most attributes of social status and the shifting of social prestige.

The social restructuring was implemented by the following main actions.

1. Immediately after the war a large-scale confiscation of property of traitors and collaborators, including the ousted Germans, was initiated. This might have amounted to about a quarter, or slightly more, of national wealth at that period. This estimate is very rough, as with the exception of land there are no adequate statistical data at our disposal.

Confiscated land made up 23·1 per cent of the acreage of the whole State. In the Czech Lands it amounted to slightly more than 30 per cent (32 per cent of agricultural land and 31 per cent of forests and other land) and in Slovakia to slightly more than 10 per cent (9·5 per cent of agricultural land, 12 per cent of forests and other land).[1]

The land confiscated was distributed among 223,000 Czech and 80,000 Slovaks, mainly peasants and agricultural labourers;[2] as a result of this the latter category largely disappeared from the interior of Bohemia and Moravia. A similar transfer of property to the benefit of the poor strata of population occurred also in the newly resettled cities in formerly German areas. It is, however, hardly possible to evaluate the magnitude of these latter changes.

2. The first phase of nationalisation, proclaimed on 28 October 1945, affected between 60 and 70 per cent of industry, especially large-scale enterprises.[3] This may have amounted to about a fifth of the national wealth.[4] According to other

---

[1] *Průběh plnění dvouletého hospodářského plánu, 1947–48* (Prague, 1949) p. 133.
[2] Ibid.   [3] *25 let Čeckoslovenska, 1945–70* (Prague, 1970) p. 71.
[4] With respect to the author's prewar estimate of national reproducible wealth, in *Review of Income and Wealth (1968)* p. 262.

sources covering the effects of both the above-mentioned
measures as shown in individual sectors of economy, the
percentages are as shown in Table 3.

Table 3

EXTENT OF SOCIALISATION IN 1947
(SHARES OF THE NATIONAL, GOVERNMENT AND
CO-OPERATIVE ENTERPRISES)

Branch	Percentage	Units of Evaluation
Transport	93·0	Employees
Industry	78·0	Employees
Forestry	62·0	Acreage
Commerce	29·9	Turnover
Handicraft	28·9	Turnover
Construction	9·0	Production costs
Agriculture	1·1	Acreage

Source: *Industry, Statistical Bulletin* (1949) p. 185, otherwise R. Lavička,
  J. Toman, *Nová organizace plánování národního hospodářství* (Prague, 1959)
  p. 6.

3. The first monetary reform; it started on 1 November 1945
with the exchange of notes and coins up to 500 Kčs, and with
freezing of money deposits to which all cash above the mentioned level should be added. These first steps were followed by
a general but strongly differentiated increase in incomes and
prices to about three times the prewar level on average. In
relation to the immediate pre-reform period the rate of increase
was much less than that in the Czech Lands (about 75 per cent);
in Slovakia about 25 per cent.[1] The reconstruction of incomes
from employment was in favour of lower incomes, in favour of
wages as compared with salaries, and of wages in agriculture in
comparison with wages in industry; the reconstruction of prices
was to the benefit of animal production and to the disadvantage
of income from property, especially rents, which were frozen at
the pre-reform level after having been kept at an almost constant
level during the war, i.e. about one-fifth higher than before the

[1] Vavro Šrobár, *Státní hospodaření za války a po revoluci*, ed. Ministry of
Finance (Prague, 1946) pp. 362–3.

war. War rationing of goods was kept and also price control. However, the system continued to be much more effective in the Czech Lands than in Slovakia, as was the case during the war.[1] The main shifts resulting from the reconstruction of wage/price relations can be seen from the indices in Table 4 comparing levels of real income with the prewar levels.

Through the increase of prices further above the level attained at the end of the war, deposits were further devaluated. Compared with the value at about the middle of the war period, the deposits were devaluated to about a half of that value. In addition to this, they were frozen, and the right to their disposition was limited. The freezing of deposits was not only an anti-inflationary measure, to neutralise the pent-up demand which might have produced continuous growth of prices, but also a means of redistribution of private property. A general single levy and a higher and progressive levy on increase of property during the war was introduced. On the other hand, freeing of certain amounts of one's own deposits was allowed in emergency cases or even regularly for legitimate reasons such as for the benefit of the old and sick.

From the total amount of about 240,000 millions of frozen primary deposits (this sum equals approximately the 1947 G.N.P. in current prices), there was, on 31 August 1948, 46,541 millions freed and about 40,000 millions due to confiscation; to the end of 1948 23,240 millions was paid in property levies.[2] Further development of these assets has not been disclosed. It is also not possible to divide these assets according to the socio-economic groups.

4. In addition to the redistribution of the confiscated land (mainly in the frontier territories) the agrarian reform which had already been performed after World War I was revised. Within this measure an additional 13 per cent of agricultural land was confiscated (the same percentage for the Czech Lands as for Slovakia), and redistribution to about 73,000 individuals (families). As a result of all these changes, the number of agricultural enterprises decreased by almost 13 per cent, but the number of medium-sized enterprises (with tenure of

---

[1] Jaromír Dolanský, *Výklad k rozpočtu na rok 1949*, ed. Ministry of Finance (Prague, 1949) pp. 168, 169 and 126.

[2] Dolanský, *Výklad*, pp. 168, 169 and 126.

Table 4

REAL INCOME INDICES IN 1946

Czech Lands (1937=100)				Slovakia (1938=100)		Czechoslovakia (1937=100)		Czechoslovakia (1939=100)	
Wages		Salaries		Wages	Salaries	Workers' pensions	Employees' pensions	Agriculture	Industry
Men	Women	Men	Women						
121	129	67	82	110	78	185	55	177	95

Source: *Průběh plnění*, pp. 330, 331, 338 and 355.
As previously stated however, there had already been an increase of prices during the war, implementing the shifts within the income structure so that the change was not so abrupt as indicated in the table. Nevertheless, the intensity of regrouping resulted mainly from the reform. Its scope and incidence is shown in Table 5.

15–20 ha.) increased by more than 20 per cent.[1] Otherwise there was no conspicuous reshuffle of land tenure structure by size, as may be seen from Table 6. The land reform should have continued in 1949 but this trend of development was soon replaced by the collectivisation campaign, as will be shown later on.

Table 5

INCOME DIFFERENTIALS AND CONCENTRATION RATIO
(CZECH LANDS ONLY)

Indicator	Prewar (1937 or 1939)	1946	1948
Differential ratios*:			
Salary/wage	253	145	134
Men/women (wages and salaries)	182	155	157
Fully skilled†/unskilled workers (wages only)	169	142	138
Industry/agriculture (wages only)	290	155	145
Highest/lowest paid industrial branch‡ (wages only)	193	166	168
Gini's coefficient of concentration	0·22871	0·17984[1]	

* Second category = 100.
† Defined as those who have worked for a required period (usually three years) as apprentices and passed the required examinations.
‡ In 1939: printing and textile industry; in 1946 and 1948: mining and confectionery industries.
[1] 1947.

Sources: Ratios, *Průběh plnění*, pp. 321, 325, 330, 331, 338 and 341.
Gini's Coefficient – Jan Zvánovec, 'Theorie koncentrace a její aplikace na důchodové rozdělení', in *Statistický Obzor*, XXIX (1949) pp. 342–52. (The higher the coefficient, the more unequal the income distribution.)

5. The second phase of nationalisation, declared after February 1948, extended nationalisation to all enterprises with more than fifty employees or fifty hectares of land (in agriculture). In the same year the single levy on property was extended to the so-called 'millionaires' levy'. Whereas the second wave of

[1] *Průběh plnění*, pp. 132–3.

nationalisation brought another additional part of industry into the socialised sector, there remained little scope for those who might have been taxed by a millionaires' levy. Towards the end of 1948 it resulted in slightly more than 1,100 million Kčs.[1]

Table 6

LAND TENURE STRUCTURE

Enterprises in Hectares	Percentage of Acreage	
	1930	1948
0–1	3·5	3·4
1–2	11·2	10·6
2–5	16·0	18·8
5–10	13·8	16·0
10–20	16·0	18·8
20–50	13·2	8·4
50 and above	26·3	24·0

Source: 25 let *Československa*, p. 107.

However, the second wave of nationalisation did not stop with the above-mentioned legal measure. It was followed by the gradual nationalisation of the remaining private industrial and commercial enterprises, mainly by confiscation because of alleged tax evasion, illicit hoarding of material and similar offences. In this rather roundabout way all private business was liquidated by about 1960.

In 1948 there were in Czechoslovakia 383,000 small handi-craft, commerce and other service enterprises in private ownership (craftsmen and tradesmen) with 905,000 working persons. These enterprises were not nationalised by the bill of 1948. Nevertheless in 1956 but 47,000 units remained with 50,000 people engaged.[2]

There were also confiscations of property which belonged to persons who emigrated after February 1948, and to those imprisoned or administratively punished for political reasons.

[1] Dolanský, *Výklad*, p. 128.
[2] Zdeněk Deyl, Antonín Kerner, 'Postavení pracovníku městských služeb v ČSSR', in *Sociální struktura socialistické společnosti*, ed. P. Machonin (Prague, 1966) p. 519.

6. The second monetary reform of 1 June 1953, combined the exchange of notes and coins with the new (deflated) price/wage relations and a further redistribution or confiscation of wealth. Unlike the first monetary reform, which had frozen the pent-up demand and then tried to decide on the frozen claims selectively, according to the social evaluation of each individual case, the second monetary reform, performed according to the instructions of Soviet experts, hit all categories of the population. It established a double, highly discriminating rate of conversion for claims of the society (goverment, national enterprises, etc.) and those of the population as far as they exceeded a certain limited amount. The basic conversion ratio of 5 Kčs of the old for 1 Kčs of the new currency was introduced for all claims from employment including pensions and other social benefits, for all claims of government and socialist enterprises, and for cash balances up to 300 Kčs of the new currency. For all other private cash balances and all other claims of individuals to the Government and Socialist enterprises the conversion ratio was stated at 50 : 1, which meant a 90 per cent confiscation.

Savings deposits in pre-1945 currency were completely annihilated. Savings deposits in post-1945 currency (i.e. after the first monetary reform) were, as a reward for the trust in currency, converted on the basic ratio 5:1 for deposits up to 5,000 Kčs and higher deposits were converted by a progressively deteriorating ratio.

Rationing was abolished, and unified prices somewhat higher than former rationed prices but lower than former free (legal market) prices, deflated by the ratio 5:1, were introduced. This put up the cost of living index of families buying only rationed goods by about 10 per cent.[1] On the other hand lower wages and salaries and also wages of some categories of workers such as in mines and industry were increased by several per cent, so that in these categories the cost of living increase was somewhat offset.

As no statistical information on the scope of the second monetary reform has been given, we can only guess very approximately the amount of savings which had been either converted or confiscated. According to the Report on the Two-

[1] *Economic Survey of Europe in 1953, E.C.E.* (Geneva, 1954) p. 64.

Year Plan the deposited savings at the end of 1949 amounted to 36,100 million Kčs. At the end of 1953 the savings deposits stood at 3,000 million Kčs. As it is reasonable to suppose only a slight increase in savings between the monetary reform on 1 June 1953 and the end of the year, it might be inferred that this sum represents approximately the sum of converted former deposits. These, if growing at the same rate as in 1949 (a year of low saving activity), might have attained at 31 May 1953, at a very careful estimate, circa 45,000 million Kčs. Then the average conversion ratio would be about 15:1 and the confiscation ratio about two-thirds.[1] The amount of confiscated cash assets is still more difficult to evaluate. The official estimates of hoardings are available only for 1947 and 1948 when they were assessed at 5,100 and 16,600 million Kčs respectively.[2] Supposing the rate of hoarding in the following years at the magnitude of an average of the above-mentioned figures, the hoarded money could amount at 31 May 1953 to about 60,000 million Kčs. These, reduced by the conversion ratio of 50:1, would leave 1,200 million Kčs to the owners.

Unfortunately, it is impossible to assess the impact of the above-mentioned confiscations on the different groups of the population. However, as only the deposits in savings banks were treated more leniently, judging from the reaction of the population in different parts of the country, we may reasonably infer that this reform hit not only the former capitalists but also the workers who especially in the privileged branches of industry such as mining, metallurgy and heavy engineering had accumulated large savings. The workers' demonstrations in several cities especially in Plzeň bear witness to this fact.[3] As Czechoslovakia had to follow Soviet Russia in all her steps on the road towards socialism, she had also had her 'Kronstadt' rebellion, however in milder 'economic' terms.

The social group which was apparently the hardest hit by the

---

[1] J. M. Michal, *Central Planning in Czechoslovakia* (Stanford, 1960) p. 140, gives a higher figure (75 per cent), however without details on the method of the estimate.

[2] *Průběh plnění*, p. 308.

[3] However, the official propaganda insisted that the demonstrations were instigated by capitalist elements. Thus in Plzeň, where, incidentally, they owned houses on the main square where the demonstrations took place, their property was confiscated and they had to move out of the city.

second monetary reform were the peasants. Most inclined to hoarding and least favoured by the change of prices, they lost most of their liquid assets and their share of the national income also decreased. Their economic independence and self-assertion were shattered and they were, in a way, preconditioned to resist less vigorously the collectivisation campaign which had been under way since 1950.

7. The collectivisation of agricultural land was the last major step in the series of measures taken to abolish private ownership to the means of production and thus to equalise wealth and socio-economic status. As the proportion of agricultural income was already low in comparison with the period immediately after the war and as the greatest inequalities in the land tenure were on the way to being abolished by the continuation of the agrarian reform, this was a measure aimed at the completion of the change of the mode of production rather than a means of redistributive justice.

Collectivisation was performed by the usual stick and carrot practice starting with persuasion, which, if not successful, changed into pressure and menaces and eventually led to the imprisonment of the most recalcitrant. In 1956 almost a half of the agricultural land was in socialist ownership (co-operatives, state farms and other government property). In 1960 this share reached 88 per cent, including the permitted private plots of co-operative farmers, amounting to about 5 per cent of the total acreage.

Collectivisation was more thoroughgoing in Czech Lands than in Slovakia. On the eve of the Prague Spring, at the turn of 1967 and 1968, the proportion of the total agricultural land left in private hands was almost 15 per cent in Slovakia whereas in the Czech Lands it was above 5 per cent only.[1]

This private land, however, is for the most part not farmers' land. The average holding being 0·8 ha. (0·5 in the Czech Lands and 1·2 ha. in Slovakia), the owner has to derive his main income from other sources.[2] According to an investigation in the middle fifties less than a quarter of holders of these dwarf

[1] CS *Statistical Yearbook* (1968) p. 304.
[2] According to the last sufficiently detailed data (at 1 January 1966) only 9 per cent of the private holdings were above 2 ha. (CS *Statistical Yearbook*, 1967, p. 285).

farms declared their total income to be mainly derived from their farming.[1] Men usually work in industry or elsewhere, whereas women take care of the land. Even of those whom the official statistics consider as private farmers (154,000 in 1968, of which 114,000 in Slovakia), 68·5 per cent were women. Taking only men into account (53,000) we may conclude that, in 1968, of 795,000 private agricultural holdings in Czechoslovakia, scarcely 7 per cent can be envisaged as farmers' family holdings.[2]

Dwarf farming, subsidiary to other economic activity, was not affected by the collectivisation. This can be seen from Table 7, showing the increased development of the structure of private agricultural holdings (enterprises) by size. In the Czech Lands, as in Slovakia, the number of agricultural holdings below 2 ha. was, in 1966, almost the same as in 1948; on the other hand, of holdings above 2 ha. only 4 per cent in the Czech Lands and 18 per cent in Slovakia remained in private ownership. Most of them were below 10 ha. In the whole of Czechoslovakia 736,000 individuals farms were collectivised.

The only substantial item of the national wealth which remained largely in private ownership were living houses, comprising 24 per cent of the value of the whole reproducible wealth in 1955. Of the total value of living houses in that year 53·6 per cent were in private ownership. This included quite a number of apartment houses which, unless the owners had fallen under expropriation measures for other reasons, remained in private ownership.[3] However, as a result of the first monetary reform which in this respect was reinforced by the second one, ownership of such apartment houses provided for the owner no advantages: on the contrary, they had mostly to be operated at a loss. Whereas the cost of construction and also of repair and maintenance were continually increasing, rents remained frozen to 1945 level, which was only about a fifth

[1] Bohuslav Šedivý-Miroslav Zubina ,'Drobní držitelé půdy a jejich úloha v našem hospodářství', in *Nová mysl*, XIV (1960) p. 80.

[2] Numbers of private farmers are taken from CS *Statistical Yearbook* (1970) p. 124.

[3] According to Kaplan's estimate there were in 1946 10,518 private owners of apartment houses in the Czech Lands and 1,315 in Slovakia. For details see Karel Kaplan, *Znárodnění a socialismus* (Prague, 1968) pp. 99 and 134.

Table 7

PRIVATE AGRICULTURAL HOLDINGS BY SIZE
(IN THOUSANDS)

Size of holdings in hectares	Czech Lands				Slovakia			
	1930	1949	1956	1966	1930	1949	1956	1966
Less than 2	508	464	550	458	171	231	276	248
2–5	278	195	123	10	126	156	133	38
5–10	145	149	90	6	95	106	72	17
10–20	95	119	48	2	45	40	12	3
20–50	46	28	3	—	11	8	—	—
Over 50	8	7	—	—	7	4	—	—
Total	1,080	962	814	476	455	545	493	306
(of which holdings over 2 ha.)	572	498	264	18	284	314	217	58

Sources: *Statistical Bulletin* (1950) p. 46; CS *Statistical Yearbooks*, 1957 (p. 114) and 1966 (p. 285).

higher than before the war. The staggering magnitude of the
differences between the development of construction costs on
one hand and rent on the other can be seen from Table 8.

Table 8

PRICE/COST RATIO IN DWELLINGS

	1937	1948	1966	1968
Construction cost	100	497*	147†	205‡
Rent	100	125[1]	36[1]	37[1]

* Official index of construction cost in Prague, corrected according to the
  Two-Year Plan Report (*Průběh plnění*, pp. 253–4).
† Implicit price index (computed as a ratio of the two official indices of
  investment in building: in current and in constant prices).
‡ Extrapolation by the official index of construction cost, reintroduced
  since 1966.
[1] Official index as published in *Statistical Yearbooks* throughout the period.

In 1960 the Czechoslovak Communist leadership concluded
that the systemic transformation had been brought so far that
the Czechoslovak Republic could officially be labelled a
Socialist State, the second to the U.S.S.R. in history.[1]

The changes performed up to that point abolished private
property of virtually all means of production, widely annihilated
liquid assets accumulated in pre-1945 and pre-1953 currency,
and to a large extent levelled the distribution of income. The
process of these changes in quantitative terms is reviewed in
synoptic tables (9, 10 and 11) and in a graph.

Table 9 covers the development of fixed assets. It shows
separately changes in the ownership of living houses, of other
reproducible wealth (buildings, machinery and livestock) and
of agricultural land. If we take into consideration that the
private agricultural land consists virtually of small husbandry
which is, as a rule, complementary to income from other
sources, and that the property of living houses cannot bring to
the owner any proceeds, we realise that by 1960 all relevant
means of production were completely socialised.

Table 10 reviews the development of liquid assets as far as it

[1] The new constitution was promulgated on 11 June 1960.

Table 9

CHANGES IN OWNERSHIP OF FIXED ASSETS

	Capital equipment in the whole economy and government services† (in per cent of value)					Agricultural land (in per cent of area)						Living houses	
	1930	1947	1950	1955	1960	1937	1947	1950	1955	1960	1965	in per cent of flats‡ (1930)	in per cent of value (1955)
Private property	(78)	(45)	10	4	0	99·5	98·9	77·9	57·4	12·0	10·0	88·4	56·3
Co-operative property	(1)	(1)	1	5	9	—		9·1	26·7	67·5	60·2	4·3 }	43·7
State property*	(21)	(54)	89	91	91	0·5	1·1	13·0	15·9	20·5	29·8	7·3 }	

* State property includes also local government property.

† Machinery, equipment, livestock and buildings excluding dwellings (living houses). In 1937 and 1947 estimates; data for 1937 are derived from my estimate of National Reproducible Wealth in 1930 (Source: *Review of Income and Wealth* (1968) p. 262); data for 1947 are derived from different sources. All other data from CS *Statistical Yearbooks*.

Co-operative property includes private plots of co-operative farmers; they amounted to 1·6 per cent of the total agricultural land in 1955, to 4·8 per cent in 1960 and eventually declined to 4·2 per cent in 1965. Source: *Dvacet let rozvoje Československé Socialistické Republiky* (Prague, 1965) p. 103, and CS *Statistical Yearbooks* (for 1937 Yearbook 1941, p. 160).

‡ In conurbations with more than 10,000 population only. Sources 1955, CS *Statistical Yearbook* (1957) p. 292. 1930, CS *Statistical Yearbook* (1936) p. 19.

DEVELOPMENT OF LIQUID ASSETS—DEPOSITS AND HOARDINGS
(IN THOUSAND MILLION OF KČS)

	Free deposits		Blocked deposits		Hoardings
	Saving deposits	Primary deposits on current account	Saving deposits	Primary deposits on current account	
End 1937	[1]57·1	[1]15·8	—	—	·
Towards end 1945	[2]111·3*	[2]42·3†	—	—	·
Reform I. XII. 1945	Blocked	Blocked			Converted to deposits and blocked
End 1946	[1]15·2	[1]42·5	[1]163·1	[1]71·3	
End 1948	[1]33·6	[1]53·3	[3]186·0‡		[4]21·7
End 1949	[1]36·1	[2]126·8			
Reform I. VI. 1953	Converted	Converted	Annihilated	Annihilated	Annihilated
End 1953	[5]3·0	·			[2]·
End 1959	[5]17·1	·			·
End 1969	[5]53·9	·			·

· Unknown – Nil.
* Czech and Slovak inland only (without frontier districts).
† Czech inland only.
‡ 31. VIII. 1948: difference between amount to this date and the previous one equals the amount of freed deposits (48·400 million Kčs).

Source: [1] Statistical Bulletin of Czechoslovakia (1950) No. 2.   [2] Šrobár, Státní hospodaření, pp. 347 and 349.   [3] Dolanský, Výklad, pp. 168 and 169.   [4] Průběh plnění, p. 308.   [5] CS Statistical Yearbooks.

Table 11

INCOME DISTRIBUTION BY SIZE

(Individual incomes from all sources – approximate global data)
Income recipients
        quintiles   *Per cent of the sum of income*

	1930	1946	1965
Lowest fifth	2·5	3·8	6·3
Second fifth	8·5	11·0	14·0
Third fifth	16·0	18·0	19·7
Fourth fifth	26·0	24·1	25·6
Highest fifth	47·0	43·1	34·4

Sources: 1930 – Jaroslav Krejčí, *Důchodové rozvrstvení* (Prague, 1947) p. 47;
1946 and 1965 – Jiří Večerník, 'Problémy příjmů a životní úrovně v
sociální diferenciaci', in *Československá společnost*, ed. Pavel Machonin
et al. (Bratislava, 1969) p. 297.

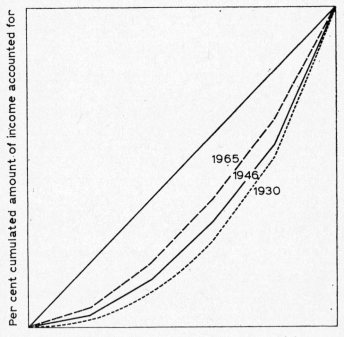

is possible on the basis of available data. It indicates the approximate amount of blocked deposits and confiscations, and the subsequent slow upsurge of new savings. We can only add that since 1945 the private savings ratio has not attained its prewar level: in 1930 savings deposits made up 6·5 per cent, in 1948 2·8 per cent, and in 1966 2·3 per cent of personal income.[1] It is of course difficult to say whether the decline in the propensity to save has its main reason only in the far-reaching levelling of personal income, or whether a shattered confidence in saving has also played its part.

Table 11 and the graph show the changes in the distribution of income by size. As data of different reliability have to be combined, only an approximate picture can be obtained. Nevertheless it allows one to draw the conclusion that a good deal of income levelling had already been performed before the postwar socialisation affected the bulk of individually owned means of production.

(D) CZECH LANDS[2] AND SLOVAKIA

In Chapter 1 (B) we have indicated how the ethnic structure of Czechoslovakia had been simplified as a result of the World War II. A virtually multinational state became a two-nation state, and this not only de facto but also de jure.[3] With some rather local exceptions the Czech–Slovak relationship became the basic ethnic issue of postwar Czechoslovakia.

Close linguistic kinship was and still is a very important link enabling easy mutual contacts of Czechs and Slovaks on any level of education. Real understanding, however, an understanding in the sense of common feeling and evaluating, has been often hampered because of a different social and cultural

[1] Percentage calculated on the basis of data for personal income and savings in Jaroslav Krejčí, 'Vývoj československého hospodářství v globální analýze', in *Politická ekonomie*, XVI (1968) p. 583–5.

[2] There is no agreed label for the Czech part of Czechoslovakia; from 1918 until 1948 it was called the Czech or 'Historical' Lands (i.e. Bohemia and Moravia-Silesia), from 1948 to 1968 the Czech regions, since 1968 the Czech Socialist Republic. However, in popular usage a newly coined term 'Česko' (Czechia), corresponding to Slovensko (Slovakia) seems to have gained some ground.

[3] Constitutional and other legal and political aspects of this change are to be dealt with in a separate book of this series.

heritage which in its turn was intimately inter-connected with a
different socio-economic structure.

The postwar policy, while in line with Marxist reasoning,
laid stress on the socio-economic differences. It was believed
that in abolishing them, i.e. in bringing Slovakia to the same
level of economic maturity as the Czech Lands, all other
differences would lose their socio-political relevance. For this
reason a faster economic growth of Slovakia became, from the
very beginning of Communist rule, one of the main targets of
economic plans.

To show how far this endeavour has been successful, sociologically relevant and statistically fairly reliable indicators have
been chosen, to characterise the following aspects of economic
maturity or, simply, modernisation: 1, urbanisation; 2, industrialisation; 3, sophistication (role of services in economy);
4, qualification of labour force; 5, mechanisation of production
(material production equipment); 6, health conditions; 7,
mechanisation of culture.

These indicators are, in Table 12, compared at ten-year
intervals, the first and last being the years of greatest political
change or highlights in Czechoslovak postwar history (1948 and
1968). In order to ease the comparison, all indicators have been
conceived in the positive sense, i.e. the higher the value, the
higher the degree of development.

Table 12 reveals what considerable progress Slovakia
achieved during the postwar period. In 1948 it was still predominantly a peasant country, with 60·2 per cent of the labour
force employed in agriculture, with only 11·5 per cent of
population in cities of over 20,000 inhabitants, with infant
mortality rate of almost 11 per cent of live births, and capital
coefficient in material production below two. In 1968, Slovakia,
although still less urbanised than the Czech Lands, was a fairly
industrialised country with high qualification of labour, a high
proportion of persons employed in services and with capital
coefficient only slightly inferior to that of the Czech Lands.[1]

[1] Capital is here understood as reproducible wealth (i.e. man-made
capital), which unlike the total wealth (including land) has, according to
available statistics from other countries, a slightly increasing tendency in
proportion to product. For details see Simon Kuznets, *Modern Economic
Growth* (New Haven and London, 1967) p. 76.

Table 12

CZECH LANDS AND SLOVAKIA. MODERNISATION RATIOS

Ratios	Czech Lands			Slovakia		
	1948	1958	1968	1948	1958	1968
1. Urbanisation (percentage of population in localities of over 20,000 population)	28·2*	30·4†	34·1	11·5*	13·6†	18·3
2. Industrialisation (percentage of labour force in mining, manufacturing and construction)	39·0	46·5	49·2	21·2	29·1	40·5
3. Sophistication (percentage of labour force in services)	26·7	28·8	34·3	16·0	24·5	32·9
4. Labour qualification (percentage of labour force with completed higher and/or secondary education)	.	9·8‡	17·2[1]	.	5·5‡	13·9[1]
5. Production equipment (fixed capital/net product ratio in the material sphere of economy)	.	2·14[2]	3·16[3]	.	1·89[4]	2·82[5]
6. Health conditions (infant vitality rate: survivors one year per 1,000 live births)	928	976	979	891	963	977
7. Culture mechanisation (radios and television sets per 1000 population)	221	309	532	67	176	351

Data on labour force do not include armed forces, employees of the Ministry of Interior and of the Party. Material sphere of economy includes mining, manufacturing, construction, public utilities, agriculture, forestry, freight transport, commerce, catering and communications serving the above mentioned industries.

* 1950.   † 1961.   ‡ 1955.   [1] 1966.   [2] 1960.   [3] 1967.

Sources: CS *Statistical Yearbooks*.

Only in the mechanisation of culture did Slovakia still lag
behind.

The change in the relative position of Slovakia to Czech
Lands can be further illustrated by the aggregate indicator.
Whereas in 1948 the Slovak per capita 'produced' material
national income was only 61·2 per cent of that in the Czech
Lands, in 1968 it attained 80·1 per cent.

This catching up by Slovakia with the economic level of the
Czech Lands results from her faster rate of growth, which as
already stated is a result of deliberate policy of the central
government, i.e. it was supported by the Czech representatives
in power. Already in the wake of the war, after the German
minority had been transferred to Germany, many factories in
the Bohemian and Moravian borderlands were dismantled and
the equipment sent to Slovakia. Since then Slovakia has always
received a somewhat larger share of investment than corres-
ponded to her share of population.

As a result of this policy the fixed capital investment per
person engaged in material production, which in Slovakia in
1948 was only 44·6 per cent of that in the Czech Lands,
attained in 1968 82·9 per cent of the Czech ratio. In industry
itself, the development of which was preferentially fostered,
Slovakia even overtook the Czech Lands. Already in 1960 her
capital equipment per worker was 4·8 per cent higher than in
the Czech Lands, and by 1968 this ratio had increased by
another 2 per cent (index ratio 106·8). On the other hand,
fixed capital assets in the non-production sphere did not develop
so fast in Slovakia. Her assets compared with the Czech Lands
increased from 48·6 per cent in 1948 to 64·4 per cent in 1968.[1]

The slower increase of investment in service industries, however, was more than matched by a faster growth in the volume
of services. Thus for example the number of population per
doctor, which in 1948 was 1,033 in the Czech Lands and 1,679
in Slovakia, attained in 1968, in both parts of the state, almost
the same level: 434 in the Czech Lands as against 480 in
Slovakia. Similarly the number of university students per member of teaching staff was, in 1948/9, 9·0 in the Czech Lands and
12·2 in Slovakia; in 1968/9 the ratio was 8·3 and 8·6 respectively.[1]

[1] Data from 25 let, p. 256.

Catching up with the Czech Lands in industrial equipment and in social services, but lagging behind in urbanisation, the Slovak population preserved greater contact with their natural environment. They also kept more to the traditional socio-cultural pattern. Thus it happened that Slovakia did not reduce her birth rate to the same extent as the Czech Lands. Because of the more favourable age composition, the mortality rate also remained lower in Slovakia. As shown in Table 13, Slovakia is still preserving her greater natural increase in population. As a result of this, Slovakia's proportion of the population of the whole state (at its postwar size) increased from 24·5 per cent in 1937 to 27·9 per cent in 1948 and 31·3 per cent in 1968. Its share of population over 60 increased from 10·0 per cent in 1950 to 13·5 per cent in 1969, whereas that of the Czech Lands increased from 12·5 per cent to 17·5 per cent.[2]

All this is producing a sociologically relevant effect, which might be, perhaps, best labelled as a shift in biological vitality. Biological vitality is a term which is not favoured by contemporary sociologists. They prefer to speak simply of the birth rate and, being concerned primarily with over-population, they do not evaluate the high birth rate positively. They are ready to admit the difficulties which are brought about by the ageing population, such as additional burden on welfare, but see them as a lesser evil easily surmountable by growing productivity, whereas the population increase, if not controlled, might endanger the very existence of the human race.

This might be true of many parts of the world, but is hardly the case with Czechoslovakia, especially the Czech Lands, and perhaps with some more countries of contemporary Europe also.[3] The Czechoslovak Population Commission, founded in 1957 with the task of discovering ways to stop the decline in the birth rate, is the best example of the awareness of the seamy side of a too cautious family planning policy.

Inadequate supply of dwellings for new families is blamed

[1] CS *Statistical Yearbooks*, 1957 and 1970.
[2] CS *Statistical Yearbook* (1970) p. 84.
[3] As so often with other phenomena in history, there appears the paradoxical situation that a rational birth-control policy is undertaken especially by those nations who, objectively, are not as much endangered by the excess of population.

Table 13

CZECH LANDS AND SLOVAKIA. VITALITY RATIOS

	Czech Lands					Slovakia				
	1945-9	1950-4	1955-9	1960-4	1965-9	1945-9	1950-4	1955-9	1960-4	1965-9
Live births per 1,000 population	21·3	19·6	15·9	14·4	14·4	25·3	28·0	24·9	20·6	18·0
Deaths per 1,000 population	13·5	11·0	10·0	10·3	11·3	14·0	10·5	8·7	7·8	8·4
Natural increase rate per 1,000 population	7·8	8·6	5·9	4·1	3·1	11·3	17·5	16·2	12·8	9·6

Source: 25 let, pp. 249–51.

most often (see p. 90) as the main reason for the birth decline. However, this is only partially true. As the difference between Slovakia and the Czech Lands indicated, it is rather a matter of urban/rural differences and also of religious attitudes.

Slovakia is not only more Catholic than the Czech Lands but what matters more, her Catholicism is less lukewarm, and therefore a more important element of everyday life.[1]

The difference between Czech and Slovak religious structure is significant also for other reasons. It has helped to mould the social climate in a special way. In this respect the Slovaks seem to be in the middle position between the Czechs and the Poles. Whereas among the Czechs the deep religious involvement of the past has been widely commuted into a strong ideological consciousness (be it with respect to National Democratic, Masarykite or Marxist tradition), the Slovaks seem to be like the Poles, more inclined to think on national lines regardless of ideological preoccupation. In Slovakia also religious behaviour is an important element of the socio-cultural structure, though not so strongly or so exclusively on Catholic lines as in Poland. A strong and culturally developed Protestant minority with traditional pro-Czech leanings and with greater acquiescence in the Communist way of life makes Slovakia a multiple rather than polarising community which seems to be characteristic of Poland. In this respect Slovakia is more reminiscent of the structure of Hungarian society, however much it lacks its traditional aristocratic features.

This study is no place to elaborate this comparison in more detail. These hints nevertheless may have been useful to indicate the special position of the Slovak socio-cultural pattern within the Eastern part of Central Europe.

Returning to the Czech–Slovak relationship itself, we may try to evaluate and compare the religious structure of the two countries. As the censuses after the war did not ask for a religious affiliation we have to rely either on data supplied by religious bodies themselves or on the results of sociological research as far as this was concerned with religious matters.

Religious behaviour and attitudes were the subject of three particular research projects in postwar Czechoslovakia. In

[1] This was proved by her people's more resolute opposition to the government repression of the Catholic Church in 1949/50.

1946 and 1947 in the Czech Lands by the Institute of Public Opinion, in 1963 in the North Moravian region on the initiative of the regional committee of the Communist Party, and in 1968 in Slovakia by the Department of Scientific Atheism in the Slovak Academy of Sciences.[1]

In addition, we can obtain quite interesting figures from a special research concerned with the social prestige of graduates in 1966. (We shall deal with this in more detail in chapter 2 E.) The questionnaire of this research contained also a question on religious affiliation. As the sample of 1,400 respondents was found in other aspects (such as socio-economic and sex structure) to be fairly representative, the same might be hoped for with respect to religious affiliation. The only way to check these results, at least indirectly, is to relate them to the last obtainable comprehensive figures and to the results of the other two researches (see Table 14). This table indicates not only the different religious structure in the two parts of Czechoslovakia but also the different gap between formal and real affiliation to (or membership of) the individual churches or denominations.

North Moravian results from 1963 and figures for the whole of Czech Lands in 1966 provide a very similar picture of real affiliation. (Differing results for Protestant and Czechoslovak churches are due to the special regional structure of the two denominations in North Moravia). On the other hand the difference between the 1966 and 1968 research results in Slovakia are mainly due to the method of investigation.[2]

[1] Results of the North Moravian investigation are summed up in Erika Kadlecová, *Sociologický výzkum religiozity Severomoravského kraje* (Prague, 1967); the Slovak research is dealt with in Peter Prušák, K niektorým výsledkom prieskumu religiózity na Slovensku', in *Sociológia* (1970) No. 1.

[2] The striking difference however, is less real than apparent. In the 1966 research, which was concerned with other issues, the religious affiliation was questioned only incidentally. Respondents were not supposed to ponder much on the reply of this question. For the 1968 research religious or nonreligious attitudes were the only subject matter. Respondents were induced to a greater concentration on that particular issue and had to state whether they believed in the main tenets of their religion, whether they are outright atheists or whether they are undecided. Only those who declared themselves as believers were listed as Catholics, Protestants, etc. They amounted to 70·7 per cent of the total number of respondents (1,265 out of 1,400 questioned). The rest consisted of atheists – 14·1 per cent and undecided – 15·2

(*continued on p. 36*)

CZECH LANDS AND SLOVAKIA. RELIGIOUS AFFILIATION
(IN PER CENT OF TOTALS IN THE RESPECTIVE YEARS)

Denomination	Czech Lands Formal affiliation — Censuses		Estimate	Czech Lands Real affiliation Samples		Slovakia Formal affiliation — Censuses		Slovakia Real affiliation Samples	
	1921	1930	1947	North Moravia 1963	Czech Lands 1966	1921	1930	1966	1968
Roman Catholic	81·9	78·5	75·7	44	44·1	70·9	71·6	65·5	57·6
Greek Catholic	0·1	0·1	0·1	—		6·5	6·4	18·8	12·7
Protestant	4·0	4·7	4·8	9	2·6	17·6	16·7	0·2	—
Czechoslovak	5·2	7·3	10·7	4	6·1	—	0·4	1·9	0·1
Orthodox	0·2	0·2	0·2	1	—	0·3	0·3	1·7	0·2
Other Christian	0·1	0·3	0·4		0·8	—			0·1
Jews	1·3	1·1	0·1		—	4·5	4·1		
Without a professed religion,	7·2	7·8	8·0	42	46·4	0·2	0·5	11·9	14·1
of which atheists*	.	.	.	30	.	.	.	.	.

— Nil or negligible.

· Not reported.

* Although atheists may appear among declared members of religious denominations, their number is related to the last group because there is their main core.

Sources: Censuses, CS *Statistical Yearbooks*; estimate on the basis of reports from churches according to the *Statesman Yearbooks* and *World Christian Handbook 1962* (London, 1962) p. 201; as data were supplied mainly by churches operating in the Czech Lands, only estimates for this part of the state were feasible; North Moravian sample 1963, Erika Kadlecová, *Sociologický výzkum religiozity Severomoravského kraje* (Prague, 1967) p. 204; comprehensive sample 1966, V. Brenner and M. Hrouda, in *Sociologický časopis*, III (1967) p. 547; Slovak sample, Peter Prušák, 'K niektorým výsledkom prieskumu religiózity na Slovensku', in *Sociológia* (1970) No. 1.

Even if we envisage only the latter results, less favourable for
religious attitudes, we realise that in Slovakia the real religious
affiliation ascertained by the samples is still in a higher proportion to the formal affiliation than in the Czech Lands.

Slovak data are interesting also in another respect. The data
for 1966 indicate that the official pressure on the Greek
Catholics in East Slovakia to accept allegiance to the Orthodox
Church was not too successful. From the 250 to 300,000 Greek
Catholics only a quarter seem to have considered themselves
as Orthodox in 1966. Data in 1968 reveal that the overwhelming
majority of those who had become Orthodox in the fifties
returned to Catholicism when they had the option.

Both striking and revealing is the difference between the
numbers of persons without a professed religion in the Czech
Lands and in Slovakia. As an interesting corollary to this the
proportion of the Communist vote in the 1946 election may be
remembered: in the Czech Lands the Communists acquired
40·17 per cent, in Slovakia 30·37 per cent of the valid vote. In
Slovakia religious affiliation was, apparently, felt to be less
incompatible with adherences to, or support of, Communist
policy. On the other hand, however, Party membership in
Slovakia also required less compromising attitudes. Towards
the end of August 1948 membership of the Communist Party
reached 25·9 per cent of the whole population in the Czech
Lands and only 13·3 per cent in Slovakia.[1]

In evaluating the figures for the sixties we have of course to
bear in mind that from 1948, when the State Board for Church
Affairs started to operate, there was a strong pressure especially
on the school population and people in government employment and in leading posts elsewhere to quit churches and to
stop practising religious life.

In the Czech Lands, where membership of the main religious
bodies was more lukewarm than in Slovakia, this pressure was
more successful: on the other hand it stiffened the attitude of
those who really adhered to religious principles, although they
were often compelled for 'existential' reasons to conceal their
beliefs and religious practices.

---

per cent. The latter might have been in the 1966 research listed as church
adherents rather than persons without a professed religion.

[1] *Dějiny Československa v datech* (Prague, 1968) p. 379.

In general it may be said that the church which was least successful in resisting both the corroding influence of secularisation (which had been in progress since the nineteenth century) and the government pressure was the Czechoslovak Church operating virtually only in the Czech Lands. Founded in 1920 as a belated attempt to restore the Hussite heritage and having combined it with a modern theology, on the lines of the Unitarians in the West, this religious body had to rely more on nostalgic or national feelings than on a genuine religious reawakening. Churches with genuine tradition and firm roots in the countryside were better equipped to hold their own, although their membership also relaxed in their beliefs.[1]

According to the Research in North Moravia the question 'Do you believe in God?' was answered in the affirmative without any reservation by 64 per cent Protestants, by 60 per cent Catholics and by 26 per cent members of the Czechoslovak Church; blankly negative answers to this question were given by 10 per cent of Catholics and Protestants equally and by 35 per cent of the members of the Czechoslovak Church. On the other hand, of people without a professed religion 4 per cent declared that they believed in God and 5 per cent admitted his existence. Questions concerning other religious attitudes were responded to in roughly similar proportions.[2]

In realising the decline of religious attitudes among the members of established churches we have not to overlook that there are throughout the whole of Czechoslovakia small religious bodies operating outside the main streams of Christianity such as Jehovah's Witnesses or Adventists, the members of which are not only very staunch but also active in missionary work. This brought them often into conflict with the state

---

[1] In the particular circumstances Protestants had some advantages over Catholics. Protestant churches being in essence national, i.e. autonomous bodies, were not so much suspected of international dependence and commitments; therefore they were less exposed to government pressure. On the other hand, having concentrated a great deal of their religious education on the churches (Sunday school) they could not be so easily hit by the abolition of religious education in the schools, which after 1948 were exclusively state schools. Finally, the Protestant churches were as a rule, less vulnerable because of the greater participation of the laity in their organisation and the greater autonomy of their congregations.

[2] E. Kadlecová, *Výzkum religiozity*, pp. 237 and ff.

authorities. In the case of the former, the main offence was the rejection of military service; in the second, observance of the Sabbath was the main stumbling block. During the fifties forced labour was often imposed on people belonging to these religious communities both in the Czech Lands and Slovakia. There, undaunted, they continued their missionary work whereby they often had to compete with Catholic priests imprisoned because of opposition to the state interferences in church affairs.

This however, can be dismissed as a marginal phenomenon. More important is that the decline of traditional forms of religious life seem not to bring a proportional rise of atheist convictions. This results from both the North Moravian and Slovak research. According to the former, 40 per cent; according to the latter, 15 per cent of adult population were undecided. Here again the difference between a Czech region and Slovakia is significant.

Although the data concerning religious attitude or affiliation are scanty, they nevertheless confirm the generally held view that Slovakia remained a more traditionally religious country than the Czech Lands. On the other hand, Slovakia's greater biological vitality and – what cannot be proved by figures but only by experience – the more emotional temperament of her people provided her with prerequisites for a more self-asserting attitude within the Czechoslovak community.

In general it may be inferred that the gradual closing of the gap between the Czech Lands and Slovakia in socio-economic development and general cultural level was not followed by a corresponding narrowing of differences in political attitudes and national awareness. It was especially not followed by reduced sensitivity of Slovak national consciousness. On the contrary, as Slovakia advanced nearer to the level of the Czech Lands, the more her intelligentsia was eager to get rid of Czech patronage and to acquire an equal footing also in the other major aspects of social life, especially the same degree of collective political self-assertion. How this endeavour culminated in the late sixties is reported in other books of this series.[1]

[1] See especially Vladimir V. Kusin, *Political Grouping in the Czechoslovak Reform Movement.*

CHAPTER TWO

New Stratification Pattern—
Status Components

In the chapter 1(C) the main measures resulting in the simplification of socio-economic patterns and the equalisation of status during the systemic transformation of Czechoslovak society have been reviewed and their impact in global terms has been quantitatively assessed.

In this chapter we shall analyse in more detail the impact of these measures on different socio-economic groups and try to indicate how far the equalisation was achieved, or prevented, by other elements of differentiation. We shall try to follow separately the individual elements or characteristics of social status and by means of them to assess the main socio-economic differentials and to identify the new pattern of stratification or formation of socio-economic groups.

We may take as the guiding line of our investigation the basic ideas put forward by W. L. Warner[1] who sums up the main characteristics of social status under the six headings which, redefined and rearranged according to our purpose and socio-cultural environment, are as follows:

1. Source and type of income and the legal conditions of employment connected with it (whether the income is derived from ownership, from employment or from social insurance, and if from employment, whether there is a differentiation between wage and salary earners);

2. Type of occupation (branch of economic activity and type of complexity of work);

3. Amount and type of education (with special regard to work qualification);

4. Amount of income (individual and households');

[1] W. L. Warner, with M. Meeker and K. Ellis, *Social Class in America* (New York, 1960) p. 163.

5. Current consumer expenditure pattern;

6. Personal wealth, especially the size and amenities of housing conditions, including area of community lived in (whether urban or rural) and ownership of consumer durable goods.

To this we may add:

7. Style of life (especially with respect to cultural values and spending of leisure time);

8. Degree of social prestige;

9. Sense of social security and possible future prospects (an element of anticipation in social status); and last but not least

10. Position within the power structure which under circumstances may become the pivotal element of the status.

Of all these ten components (or attributes) of social status only one – the source of income – directly reflects the relationship to the means of production, i.e. the class position in the Marxist sense. It is obvious that socialisation of the means of production *per se* does not necessarily imply the abolition of differences in other components of status. To achieve this, other criteria have to be envisaged and other means applied. This is the more obvious as the tendency towards what sociologists call 'decomposition of attributes of status' becomes widespread in industrial societies irrespective of their socio-economic formation.[1]

In Chapter 1 (C) we have already indicated several measures aimed at greater equalisation within the society, measures taken independently of the socialisation of the means of production. On the following pages we shall return to them in more detail. Our discussion, however, will be focused on the stratification pattern in general.

(A) TYPE OF INCOME AND OCCUPATION BY INDUSTRY

After the process of socialisation had been completed, there remained, with the exception of fees and royalties of officially acknowledged authors and artists, no other legal source of sizeable income except employment (present, such as wage and

[1] See W. Wesolowski, 'The Notions of Strata and Class in Socialist Society', in *Social Inequality*, ed. André Béteille (London, 1969) pp. 128–33.

salary, or past, such as pensions) or membership of a collective farm. The share of population living predominantly from wages or salaries increased from 64·1 per cent in 1930 to 72·8 per cent in 1950. In 1961 it reached 85·4 per cent, and in 1968, 89·1 per cent.

Within this category there was, before the war, a wide gap between the workers (wage earners) and other employees (salary earners). This gap consisted not only in the average level of income (as shown earlier) but in a whole series of legal provisions which made the position and consequently also the social status of the salary earners more advantageous. An employee was paid on a monthly basis (a worker on a weekly basis), had slightly shorter working hours, was entitled to two to four weeks' paid holiday (workers only to one or two weeks) and enjoyed a better social insurance scheme, both with respect to sickness benefits and treatment and with respect to old age pensions.

Main legal differences were abolished between 1945 and 1948. Then a comprehensive national insurance scheme covered all workers and other employees indiscriminately and similarly a new labour code recognised no difference of the above-mentioned kind between manual and non-manual workers. In addition, as shown in Table 5, the differentials between average salary and average wage decreased considerably: from two and a half before the war to less than one and a half in 1946, and to one and a third in 1948.

Thus several important elements of social differentiation disappeared and made the mass of those who earned their income from employment more homogenous with respect to this particular element of status. In the living standard however, as will be shown later on, this homogenisation was reflected in the basic material consumption such as food and basic industrial goods rather than in the consumption of cultural goods and services and the style of life connected with this.

Since this difference, which in its turn is a function of the amount and type of education, has held sociological relevance until recently, it is advisable to retain in our further investigation the division of the labour force according to the manual or non-manual type of work (blue and white collar workers respectively) as far as the available statistics allow it. However,

in comparing these data with those from before the war, we
have to bear in mind that the socio-economic difference,
especially with respect to the income and legal attributes of the
status, decreased considerably.

Similarly, the position of co-operative producers outside
agriculture does not differ materially from that of workers and
other employees in the state enterprises. Members of non-
agricultural co-operatives are in all respects treated as employees. Their participation in the co-operative ownership
entitles them only to an additional compensation distributed at
the end of each year according to the economic results, a compensation which, however, equals as a rule only a portion of the
monthly salary. Other membership rights are a pure formality.

The only sociologically different category are peasants, be
they co-operative (as a rule) or independent (a negligible
minority). Although the ownership rights of the member of an
agricultural co-operative do not substantially differ from those
in non-agricultural co-operatives, nonetheless the existence of
permitted private plots, the type of work, rural environment,
and less developed Communist Party organisation puts the
members of agricultural co-operatives into a better position
vis-á-vis their superiors who cannot manipulate the decision-
making within the seemingly democratic statutory framework
so easily as in urban, manufacturing or services supplying co-
operatives. However, with respect to the centrally planned
economy, the scope for co-determination even so remains very
limited.

Bearing this in mind we may proceed to review the quantitative development of individual categories. The general official
presentation is reproduced in Table 15.

This table reveals some interesting trends of development
which, however, are only partly due to the systemic transformation. The change of the socio-economic formation can be
seen in the disappearance of the category of private enterprisers
(capitalists) and in the drop in the number of professionals,
small farmers, craftsmen and shopkeepers. On the other hand
the smaller number of co-operative peasants in the sixties than
of former small peasants whom they have replaced is due to the
well-known pattern of economic growth, consisting of shifts of
the labour force from primary to secondary and, eventually,

tertiary industries. Similarly the comparatively stable proportion of workers and rapidly growing proportion of other employees results from technological advance and the economic change connected with it.

Table 15

CHANGES IN THE SOCIAL STRUCTURE
IN PER CENT OF THE WHOLE POPULATION,
INCLUDING FAMILY MEMBERS

		1930*	1950	1961	1969
1	Workers	57·3	56·4	56·3	58·2
2	Other employees	6·8	16·4	27·9	29·7
3	Co-operative farmers	—	0·0	10·6	8·3
4	Other co-operative producers	—	0·0	1·2	1·1
5	Small peasants	22·2	20·3	3·5	2·2
6	Professionals	⎫	⎫	0·1	0·1
7	Small craftsmen and shopkeepers	⎬ 8·2	⎬ 3·8		
		⎭	⎭	0·4	0·4
8	Capitalists	5·5	3·1	—	—

* In the postwar territory

Source: *Statistical Yearbooks*, 1930, V. Srb, 'Obyvatelstvo Československa v letech 1918–1968', in *Demografie* (1968) p. 301.

From this point of view, the category of other employees has to be scrutinised in more detail. It has expanded both vertically and horizontally. Horizontally, the continuous growth of service industries, where traditionally white-collar workers prevailed, operates self-evidently in this direction. Vertically, in the traditionally blue-collar, i.e. goods-producing industries, the ratio of other employees to the workers had been continuously increasing since before the war. To evaluate the magnitude of this double expansion, statistics on the occupational structure have to be used. These will provide us also with the basic information on another element of social status, though only on broad lines. The official presentation of the changes in the occupational structure is reproduced in Table 16.

This table reveals a development which only partly corresponds to the prevalent tendencies in the economically advanced

countries. Czechoslovakia shared with them only the decline of
persons engaged in agriculture. On the other hand, the proportion of persons engaged in service industries as a whole (items 4,
5, 6 and 7 of the table) increased only insignificantly, and
between 1950 and 1960 even slightly declined. However,
individual branches of services developed in a very different
way. Personal and household services were reduced to a third
of the prewar level. Commercial services (banking, trade and
insurance, etc.) declined considerably. The share of transport
and communication stagnated. Only the public services increased sharply. Their share in the occupational structure more
than doubled within the thirty years reviewed.

Table 16

CHANGES IN THE OCCUPATIONAL STRUCTURE
IN PER CENT OF THE WHOLE POPULATION,
INCLUDING FAMILY MEMBERS

		1930*	*1950*	*1961*
1	Agriculture, forestry and fishing	32·9	24·9	19·3
2	Industry (mining and manufacturing)	28·8	29·1	33·8
3	Construction	5·6	5·7	8·9
4	Transport and communication	6·8	7·4	6·1
5	Trade, banking and insurance	7·0	7·1	5·3
6	Public services	5·2	8·5	10·7
7	Personal and household services	2·8	1·0	0·9
8	Persons without earning capacity	9·4	15·3	14·5
9	Not stated	1·5	1·0	0·5

* In the postwar territory

Source: V. Srb, in *Demografie*, X (1968) p. 300.

All these are characteristic features of the systemic transformation according to the Soviet pattern, remarkable by the
stress laid on heavy industry. With the liquidation of small
private enterprises a transfer of labour force from shops and
workshops to mining, metallurgy and heavy industry was
carried through. Thus there was a strong flow from the category
of self-employed to the category of workers. Its magnitude may
have amounted to about 300,000 during the fifties. Approxi-

mately another 100,000 workers were recruited from former non-manual employees and professionals.

On the other hand, there was a flow of approximately the same magnitude from the workers' category to the employees'. There was a conscious policy to promote party members of merit from manual work to positions in the State, particularly to the Party and security apparat. According to the data revealed at the General Party Conference in 1956 there were about 325,000 party members, i.e. 5 per cent of the labour force, who were at this date employees but former workers.[1] According to other official data there were, in 1960, 462,821 and in 1962, 489,436 'brain' workers (i.e. employees in jobs for which higher or secondary education was, as a rule, required), who, however, had not reached this level of education.[2] Their number was about a third of all employees described as 'brain' workers. Apparently they were mainly former workers who had been appointed to these jobs because of political merits or outstanding reliability.

In order to get a deeper insight into the development of individual groups of services we have to carry out our investigation still further. As the published statistics on occupational structure do not contain more detailed breakdowns for all years compared, we have to use statistics of persons working instead and compare their numbers either with the total labour force or the total population. As the precise total labour force actually in operation is not known (figures for army, security and Party apparats are not disclosed) the latter has to be preferred.

Because of the different ratio of persons engaged per family in primary industry on the one hand and secondary and tertiary industries on the other, this comparison supplies a more accurate picture of the labour input within the occupational structure. Further on, this approach enables us also to include some categories of persons engaged in those services, the statistics of which are not disclosed, and for which we have to

[1] This figure is derived from the percentage data of the Party members given in the former President Novotný's speech at the General Conference of the Communist Party of Czechoslovakia in June 1956. Source: Antonín Novotný, *Projevy a stati 1* (Prague, 1964) p. 349.

[2] CS *Statistical Yearbook* (1963) p. 120.

provide data from other sources and then only approximate
ones. Unfortunately, the postwar development can be compared
only with 1930, when the comprehensive census data are available.

In Table 17 the proportion of persons engaged in agriculture
is larger than in the conventional presentations because not
entire families but working individuals are counted – and these
are, in agriculture, more than one per family. The proportion of
persons engaged in agriculture thus conceived did not decrease
considerably between 1930 and 1950. This was the result of the
transfer of Germans, the proportion of whom employed in
industry and commercial services was higher than in the whole
population. Thus it happend also that the share of persons
engaged in industry and construction temporarily decreased.
Then, however, as a result of the industrialisation drive, their
numbers went up sharply. The relative number of persons
working in industry and construction still continues to increase.

The development of distribution and transport combined
fared only slightly better than in the previous presentation
(Table 16). The relative growth is conspicuous only since the
sixties. Similarly the rehabilitation of other economic services is
a phenomenon of the sixties, when preference for heavy industry
was somewhat relaxed and the planners were alarmed by the
consumers' dissatisfaction with the supply of services.

Unlike the economic services, the public services expanded
continuously, and very sharply, throughout the period. This
can be seen already from the occupational structure in Table
16. Table 17 gives a more detailed breakdown of this category,
showing the astounding differences later on. In this context we
would like to stress that the conspicuous increase of persons
engaged in education and culture, health and social care,
research and science, is a phenomenon characteristic of all
industrially advanced countries. However, with respect to
education and health, it has to be added that these activities
acquire in a socialist state of Soviet type a special, consciously
systemic connotation. The first as a means of vocational rather
than general education, and, as far as general education is
concerned, primarily as a means of ideological and consequently
(or alternatively) 'behavioural' integration or rather homogenisation; the other (health) primarily as a means of improving

Table 17

CHANGES IN OCCUPATIONAL PATTERN

Persons engaged (including regularly helping family members) per 1,000 of population

		1930*	1950	1960	1968	1969	Index 1968/30
1	Agriculture and forestry	181·5	173·9	115·0	91·2	89·9	49
2	Industry and construction	171·3	164·6	203·9	223·1	224·0	127
3	Distribution and transport†	54·1	60·7	62·0	72·1	75·9	130
4	Other economic services	17·4	11·1	12·0	20·1	20·5	113
5	Education and culture	6·1	13·2	20·9	28·3	29·1	452
6	Health and social care	3·6	8·6	13·0	17·0	17·9	444
7	Research and science	.	1·9	7·8	12·0	12·4	865[3]
8	Government administration and justice‡	6·2	13·1	7·8	7·7	8·2	123
9	Armed forces: Army (including Air Force)	11·1	.	15·2[1]	16·2[2]	.	140[2]
10	Security	1·4	.	3·2[1]	2·8[2]	.	194[2]
11	Total	452·7	.	460·8	491·0	.	106
12	Of which services (items 3–10)	99·9	.	141·9	176·1	.	171
13	Total population	1,000·0	1,000·0	1,000·0	1,000·0	1,000·0	97·5

* In the territory of that year (i.e. including Ruthenia).

† Transport, communications, trade (including catering).

‡ Excluding Ministries of National Defence and of Interior.

[1] 1962.   [2] 1966.   [3] 1940 = 100.

Sources: CS Statistical Yearbooks with the following exceptions: Research and Science in 1940 – Radovan Richta et al. Civilizace na rozcestí, 3rd ed. (Prague, 1969) p. 383; Armed forces in the postwar years: Data from Statesmen's Yearbooks checked against the statistics of persons employed, persons insured and labour force balance in CS Statistical Yearbooks.

that productive force which is represented by manpower. The less conspicuous but nevertheless considerable increase in security forces is a seamy side of the preoccupation with ideological and behavioural homogeneity.

Taking all these groups of services together, the tertiary sector shows a greater expansion than was the case in the previous presentation. The number of persons engaged in both secondary and tertiary industries increased faster than the decline in the primary industries because of the growing proportion of economically active in the whole population. This latter proportion increased from 45·3 per cent in 1930 to 49·1 per cent in 1968. This is a somewhat higher proportion than is usually given because in our presentation the armed forces are also included. The only gap which still remains is the civil apparat of the Ministry of the Interior, of the Ministry of Defence and of the Communist Party.[1]

We may now return to the other, vertical line of increase of white-collar workers. Its relative growth can be followed even from before the war. In industry (mining and manufacturing) the ratio of blue-collar workers to white-collar workers was, in 1935, 9:1 and in 1950, 5·3:1. In 1960 this ratio dropped to 4·0 and in 1969 to 3·4. However, within the categories of white-collar workers (other employees) the increase was mainly due to technical personnel, the proportion of whom in the whole labour force employed in industry increased from 10·1 per cent in 1953 to 14·2 per cent in 1969. On the other hand the share of purely administrative personnel dropped from 7·7 per cent to 5·5 per cent. In the construction industry the development was similar, the technical personnel increased from 7·8 per cent in 1950 to 10·2 per cent in 1955 and eventually 15·3 per cent in 1969. Administration personnel remained stable at about 6 per cent of the labour force employed in construction.

Unfortunately we are not able to follow this development with respect to agriculture. Nevertheless, we can infer from what we know from the fragmentary evidence that the share of white-collar workers increased also in primary production.

---

[1] In order to bring the prewar figures on to a comparable basis corresponding items were excluded from 1930 data.

(B) EDUCATION AND OCCUPATION BY LEVEL OF
TRAINING

The abolition of income from property and of legal differences between wage and salary earners had to be followed by the abolition of another important source of social inequality. It was postulated that the young generation of former proletarians should get better access to higher education. One means of achieving this was to provide all with an equal basic education. The former system of streaming after five years of elementary school attendance provided several different levels of education from the eight-year gymnasium (widely understood as preparation for university), through four years of technical education for industry, commerce, etc., to the three-year secondary school (conceived as a completion of the obligatory elementary education at a lower level). It was replaced by a comprehensive system until the fifteenth year of age. After the nine-year obligatory education, selection for further education was made dependent not only on school success but also on the social origin of parents. Preference was given to children of workers and co-operative farmers. Children from bourgeois families were admitted to higher education only in those cases when either their parents stood the test of an explicitly positive attitude towards the system, or when they themselves after having worked one or several years in industry were sent to further studies by their enterprises.

The opportunity of studying simultaneously with employment was given to large numbers by introducing evening courses (see p. 58). The grants system was also enlarged. In 1967–8 two fifths of full-time university students received a grant, however meagre in terms of the Western standard. Its average value amounted to about 4,000 Kčs per year; computed on the basis of comparative purchasing power (see p. 74) this equals £100 per year.[1]

The endeavour to overcome the socially conditioned inequalities in education went so far that everybody, unless apparently mentally subnormal, was supposed to have sufficient learning capacity to master standard elementary education

---

[1] An average grant of 1,835 Kčs per year was awarded to 11 per cent of full-time students at secondary level. (CS *Statistical Yearbook* (1969) p. 490).

stretched over nine years. Objective criteria for measuring intelligence and testing methods were distrusted as revealing socially conditioned rather than innate intelligence and accordingly banned. The Institute of Human Labour (Ústav lidské práce), engaged primarily in psychometric and testing methods, was disbanded.

Positively, the new system was intended to fulfil two aims: first, to extend vocational education and training; and second, to educate a new type of man, a socialist man, i.e. a man with other incentives for work than his own profit, a man considering as of supreme value the work for the socialist fatherland and its future, and on a higher level of education, a man accepting Marxism–Leninism as his life philosophy.

Studying was considered a matter of socialist policy rather than of personal preference or interests. Although formally no 'numerus clausus' was introduced, the number of student admissions to individual schools and departments was regulated according to the planned number of jobs in various branches of employment. Before completing their studies, students had to take care to get a card of employment (umístěnka) which on the one hand assured them a proper post and on the other was a means of filling vacancies in unattractive localities throughout the country.

In order to educate a new type of man, teaching in the humanities was focused on ideological training, and was combined with fulfilling practical duties to the society such as working in brigades, writing posters, organising collective attendance at cultural enterprises and performing mutual criticism and self-criticism. Teaching of history was centred on the modern period starting with the rise of industry and characterised by the exploitation of the working class by the capitalists. The highlights were the Workers' Movement, the Communist Party, the October Revolution, the building of socialism in Soviet Russia and the role of this country in the defeat of Fascism and in helping to introduce socialism in other countries. Earlier history was reproduced rather sketchily and interpreted as a chain of class struggles providing a picture of the continuously deteriorating fate of the toiling masses. In Czechoslovak history great stress was laid on the Hussite period, which was interpreted as a class war *par excellence*. On the other hand, the renewal of the Czech State and the foundation of the Czechoslovak Republic in 1918 was interpreted as a result of forces put into motion by the October Revolution in Russia rather than as the outcome of the defeat of the Central Powers during World War I and of the liberation movement led by T. G. Masaryk. The latter became a target of intensive vilification.

In geography, the focus was on the socialist states and the whole curriculum was conceived as a basis for teaching the advantages of these states in comparison with capitalist ones. Economics and civic education, which in the prewar curricula received only a rudimentary treatment, were expanded and used as another basis of indoctrination.

Even in the sciences the opportunity for ideological education was sought and found in stressing theories of Soviet and Russian scientists, allegedly based on or confirming the philosophy of dialectical materialism and/or proving the superiority of the socialist system. Biology and psychology in particular received a distorted emphasis as a result of this policy. Biology became the domain of Lysenko's voluntaristic ideas, and psychology was dominated by Pavlov's theory of conditioned reflex.

Sometimes the ideological influence was rather negative such as in the banning of sociology and cybernetics as bourgeois pseudo-sciences. Even physics did not escape this fate. Einstein's theory of relativity was a taboo during the fifties. On the other hand, in all universities Marxism–Leninism was introduced as an obligatory subject for all types of curricula in which all students had to pass the examination.

All this of course put extra ideological demands on teachers, whose political reliability was continuously tested and improved by briefing; those who did not follow the line were purged. The endeavour was to achieve within the different levels of mental capacity a satisfactory ideological homogenisation of the next generation.

How far this expectation was met by success, especially the students' reaction and the subsequent development of Marxism–Leninism departments from safeguards of orthodoxy in the fifties into focuses of heresy in the sixties, will be briefly reviewed in the last chapter. Within this context we would like only to state that during the early sixties the banned disciplines were gradually readmitted and, at the university level, greater objectivity was observed.

The new school system eased the natural drive for higher education, which is a general phenomena all over the world. It opened to a greater extent the door of higher education to members of the lower strata. On the other hand it banned from higher education children not only from former bourgeois families but also children of political non-conformists, such as people with strong religious convictions and especially those who were sentenced because of anti-state activity all without respect to the class origin. However, what was still worse in the long run was the lowering of the standard of education at the senior level. This was due not only to the necessity of adapting the single, undifferentiated curriculum to the less well-endowed pupils, but also to the greater stress on the political reliability than on the special qualifications of the teachers; and last but not least, to the widespread practice of sending pupils of the secondary stage to working brigades, especially at times of harvest. Thence from the middle sixties opinions were voiced recommending the abandonment of these practices and the reintroduction of a selective system for brighter children.

It is difficult to assess the result of this school policy in quantitative terms because we have no corresponding data before 1948. However, from the statistics of students' social origin which were published from 1955/6 to 1963/4 and from the structure of school population, which is known also from before the war, we may infer that the impact of this policy was considerable.

Although the proportion of students from workers' families did not attain the percentage of workers in the whole population, it substantially increased after 1948 and continued to do so between 1955/6 and 1963/4. On the other hand the co-operative farmers' descendants got extraordinarily preferential treatment at the beginning of collectivisation, and later kept approximately in line with the proportion of their families within the whole population. The residual group, consisting almost exclusively of white-collar workers, supplied a student population far above its share in the whole population. Details are given in Table 18.

A comparison with prewar conditions can be made only with

respect to the relative weight of different types of schools in the total school population (see Table 19).

From it the following deductions can be made: (*a*) there was a considerable relative growth of school population above elementary level; (*b*) general education expanded very much at the lower level (Table 19, row 5), whereas at the higher end (row 2) it decreased; (*c*) the relative increase in higher education was to the benefit of vocational education including universities. The number of pupils in schools for apprentices (schools with part-time attendance combined with employment in the job concerned) also considerably increased; (*d*) finally, as will be demonstrated later on (Table 21), within vocational education, technical studies expanded more than preparation for other branches, especially at the secondary level.

Table 18

SOCIAL ORIGIN OF STUDENT POPULATION*
IN PER CENT OF RESPECTIVE LEVEL OF EDUCATION

Family origin (school years)	Workers		Co-operative farmers		Others	
	1955/6	1963/4	1955/6	1963/4	1955/6	1963/4
Upper secondary schools for vocational education	40·2	46·5	15·3	11·5	44·5	42·0
Upper secondary schools for general education	30·3	41·1	12·3	6·1	57·4	52·8
Universities, polytechnics and other schools of higher education	29·1	37·9	13·4	8·3	57·5	53·8
Whole population	56·3†	57·9	3·8	9·0	27·9†	33·1

* Full-time (daily) students.   † 1961.

Source: CS *Statistical Yearbooks*.

After this excursus on the basic concepts and impact of the new education system we may return to our inquiry into the relevance of the elements of social status.

If we are to tackle the problem from the point of view of special training or education for particular professions, we get the following groups: (1) specialists with higher education, (2) specialists with secondary education, (3) personnel with vocational training (skilled and semi-skilled workers), (4) personnel without vocational training or higher education (unskilled workers).

Table 19

STRUCTURE OF SCHOOL POPULATION
IN PER CENT OF TOTAL FULL-TIME SCHOOL POPULATION*

		1935/6	*1965/6*
1	Universities, polytechnics and other schools of higher education	1·1	3·1
2	Upper secondary schools for general education	5·3	3·3
3	Upper secondary schools for vocational education	3·6	6·5
4	Lower secondary (part-time) schools for vocational education (schools for apprentices)	6·6	11·2
5	Lower secondary schools for general education	16·6	33·1
6	Elementary schools	66·5	41·0
7	Schools for handicapped children	0·3	1·8
	Total full-time school population (number of persons)	2,702,770	2,998,763

* Without attendance of evening courses; kindergarten and nursery schools not included.

Source: CS *Statistical Yearbooks.*

The relative strength of these categories, at the time of complete socialisation on one hand and on the eve of the 1968 crisis on the other, is reproduced in Table 20.

Specialists with higher education form the core of what is usually called the intelligentsia. Specialists with secondary education may, under certain circumstances, be considered as also belonging to this group. As it is not possible to make any satisfactory division of the second group according to this, in any case vague, criterion (intelligentsia), we shall include both of these groups under this heading – making a distinction between upper and lower intelligentsia.

Table 20

SOCIO-ECONOMIC GROUPS BY EDUCATIONAL LEVEL
IN PER CENT OF LABOUR FORCE

	1959/60	*1966/7*
Specialists with higher education	2·6	3·7
Specialists with secondary education	10·7	13·7
Skilled personnel (with vocational training) in the state sector*	38·6	43·6
Skilled personnel in co-operative farms	13·8†	9·5
Unskilled workers	34·3	29·5
Total	100·0	100·0

* Including non-agricultural co-operatives.
† Estimate.

Computed on the basis of CS *Statistical Yearbooks*; two years have to be combined because all statistics were not available for the same year. Number of unskilled personnel is the residual item.

Both these groups of intelligentsia constitute slightly more than a half of non-manual workers or 'other employees' in the terminology of official statistics (Table 15). The other half falls into the other two categories, but predominantly into the third one, that of skilled personnel.

According to the official interpretation skilled workers (manual and non-manual), including those in agriculture, in 1959 constituted more than 40 per cent and in 1967 more than a half of the labour force. However, of the skilled personnel within the state socialist sector, only 33·3 per cent in 1959 and 36·3 per cent in 1967 worked in those professions for which they were trained.[1] This is an amazing finding, which deserves to be reviewed in more detail.

A breakdown by individual industries (Table 16) shows that in 1959 the lowest percentage of skilled labour working in jobs for which they were trained was in mining, metallurgy, the

[1] Data from CS *Statistical Yearbook* (1968) p. 135.

chemical industry and agriculture and forestry, i.e. in branches
to which either labour had to be forcibly conscripted, such as
mining and metallurgy, or which had no particular tradition of

Table 21

UTILISATION OF SKILLED LABOUR
THE PERCENTAGE OF SKILLED PERSONNEL WORKING IN
INDIVIDUAL INDUSTRIES WITH SPECIAL TRAINING
IN THAT PARTICULAR INDUSTRY

	30 November 1959	*30 September 1967*
Mining	18·4	26·8
Metallurgy	19·2	27·6
Chemical industry	14·6	25·9
Machinery and other iron-working industry	67·9	67·1
Electricity	73·8	71·4
Construction	78·3	73·9
Building material, earthenware and glass industry	31·9	23·2
Wood and musical instrument industry	63·7	45·0
Paper, printing and film industry	73·0	66·2
Textile and clothing industry	38·6	39·7
Leather and shoe industry	37·5	27·3
Food industry	55·3	43·4
Agriculture and forestry	22·3	22·2
Commerce, catering and other commercial services	54·2	67·0
All branches together	33·3	36·3

Source: CS *Statistical Yearbook* (1968) p. 135.

vocational training on the lower level such as chemical industry
or agriculture. In 1967 the position of mining, metallurgy and
the chemical industry considerably improved; on the other
hand, in several old industries such as building materials,
ceramics and glass, wood, leather, shoe and food industries, the
ratio of skilled personnel working in jobs for which they were
trained deteriorated.

Thus, in general, not much was achieved during the eight years in which these relationships can be followed.

A special problem is presented by agriculture. Complete data for several years are available only for the state sector. Data for the co-operative sector are available for 1967, when of all persons working in co-operatives 92·4 per cent were counted as skilled workers, two years continuous work in agriculture being supposed to be sufficient professional training. Although this might be plausible, it puts the category of skilled workers in co-operative farms in a better position than in the other economy. If we are to take into account only those who have passed an apprenticeship examination, our survey would include only people working in some craft related to agricultural production (they made up 14·6 per cent of all workers in agricultural co-operatives), and this would again be a wrong supposition. In view of this difficulty we have to deal with the co-operative farms as a separate item.

Unfortunately, we have no corresponding data for the actual utilisation of specialists with higher education before 1970.

Nevertheless we may obtain a fairly reliable picture from different sources, at least for the early sixties. As has been mentioned earlier (see p. 45) in 1960 and 1962 (in both cases to 30 September), more than a third of employees in jobs for which higher or secondary education was, as a rule, required did not possess this type of education. This category comprised almost half a million persons in 1962. The remaining two thirds were composed mainly of persons with secondary education (692,000 in 1960 and 777,000 in 1962), and only to a lesser extent of specialists with higher education (147,000 in 1960 and 168,000 in 1962).[1] On the other hand, according to the 1961 census (the census date was 1 March, which is only five months later than the above-mentioned 1960 data), the number of persons with higher education in the productive age range was 187,000.[2] This means that about 40,000 specialists with higher education, i.e. 27 per cent of the total, were at the turn of 1960/1 not in employment commensurate with their qualification. In 1970 there were 32,430 in that position.[3]

Thus, as a result of transfer of workers from service industries

---

[1] Source: CS *Statistical Yearbook* (1963).
[2] UN *Demographic Yearbook* (1963).   [3] CS *Statistical Yearbook* (1971) p. 142.

and agriculture to heavy industry and of people with higher
education to manual work, and, in the opposite direction, as a
result of promotion of manual workers, skilled or unskilled to
administrative jobs in apparats and management, the occupational pattern considerably diverged from the corresponding
pattern of vocational training. This was one of the main
sources of economic losses, losses in the potential of working
energy which, although uncalculable in terms of money or
other economic units, was nevertheless much in the minds of
economic reformers in the late sixties.

During the sixties a certain tendency to improve this relationship seems to have persisted. However, the percentage of skilled
personnel working in the occupation of their training increased
(as can be seen from Table 21) by only three points from 1959
to 1967. A certain pressure was exerted on former workers or
other people with inadequate professional training employed in
administrative jobs to improve their qualification by studying
at evening or part-time courses (dálkové kurzy). The attendance
of these courses greatly expanded up to the early sixties: at all
levels of education together, from 10,251 participants in 1951/2
to 189,554 participants in 1963/4, i.e. from 0·2 per cent to 3·0
per cent of the total labour force in the respective years. After
having attained its apogee in 1963/4 (at the higher level the
apogee was attained a year later), the attendance at evening
and part-time courses started slowly to decrease, until it dropped
to 111,970 participants or 1·6 per cent of labour force in 1969/70.
This trend reversal reflects both the change of employment
policy (vacant posts were filled with young intelligentsia whose
reliability was supposed ex ante, rather than with reliable
cadres from outside, whose qualification had to be acquired
additionally) and the saturation point of already employed
workers' cadres with the capacity for promotion at the qualification level.

On the other hand pressure to keep certain intellectuals out
of their professions was gradually relaxing from about 1963/4
until in 1968 the majority of them found jobs in their own
professions, although not always on the level corresponding to
their qualification. Unfortunately, since 1969, this trend has
been reversed again, especially on the cultural plane.

Meanwhile the number of people with higher education

continued to increase. In 1966 specialists with higher or secondary education (i.e. intelligentsia in the broader sense) made up 17·4 per cent of the labour force. At the earliest date of corresponding data – 1955 – there was only 8·6 per cent of intelligentsia within the labour force. The share of specialists with higher education (upper intelligentsia) also doubled; it increased, in the same period, from 1·7 to 3·4 per cent of the labour force. The share of this level students per 1,000 of population in the age group between 18 and 24 increased from 17·7 in 1936/7 to 39·6 in 1955/6 and to 57·2 in 1967/8.[1]

All this must have produced a shift in the balance of social 'vectors' within the society. People with higher education are, as a rule, more critical of their environment, especially that part of it which is somehow connected with their own occupation or field of interest. They did not accept so readily the stereotyped indoctrination pattern which was in such ample use during the whole of the fifties. However, insofar as they are in more responsible and better paid jobs, or insofar as they do not possess sufficient skill to earn more in manual work, they are more interested in whether or not they lose their jobs than are manual workers, and therefore are more inclined to opportunistic behaviour. Up to a certain age only, a tendency to nonconformity prevails. However, under the strict régime of the Communist education system any dissensions could easily acquire a certain anti-system connotation.

Nevertheless, the young generation with higher education, being in a growing proportion of working-class origin, felt more confident in expressing their opinion because they considered themselves as the representatives of the class whose ruling role in society they had been taught. They also tried to make better use of the formally democratic framework and to turn its use from window-dressing to genuine functioning. However, as the experience of students' 'majales' (unofficial May celebrations) and similar undertakings has shown the students from families of the ruling strata were especially active and critical. It was they who, knowing better the situation behind the scenes, were most of all struck by the contradictions between theory and practice in socialism.

Thus the relative weight of the intelligentsia increased not

[1] 25 let, p. 237.

only in terms of numbers but also in terms of active involvement; it was developing into a much stronger social 'vector' than could be supposed from sheer numbers.

Within the relative growth of the intelligentsia there were two sociological relevant trends to observe. First, the growing proportion of women especially on the university level, and secondly shifts in favour of technical education at both secondary and higher levels.

The share of women students in higher education increased from 20·3 per cent in 1946/7 to 40·6 per cent in 1968/9, at the secondary level of the vocational education from 45·1 per cent to 53·1 per cent (including part-time courses combined with employment, the increase was to 57·0 per cent). Projected into the structure of population by age, the proportion of intelligentsia in the male and female population was in the census year of 1961 as shown in Table 22:

Table 22

POPULATION BY SEX, AGE AND LEVEL OF EDUCATION IN 1961
IN PER CENT OF POPULATION IN THE RESPECTIVE
AGE GROUP

	Male		Female	
Age	With secondary education	With higher education	With secondary education	With higher education
15–19	11·5	—	16·9	—
20–4	25·7	1·4	29·0	1·2
25–34	21·6	6·3	20·0	2·1
35–44	20·2	8·7	16·2	1·0
45–54	12·9	3·2	10·5	0·5
55–64	10·1	2·3	7·7	0·3
65 and over	8·3	2·4	4·1	0·1
Unknown	5·5	1.6	5·1	0.4
Total (all age groups)	16·0	3·3	13·8	0·8

Census data. Source: UN *Demographic Yearbook* (1963).

Table 23

STRUCTURE OF INTELLIGENTSIA IN 1955 AND 1966

(NUMBER OF WHITE-COLLAR WORKERS WITH HIGHER AND SECONDARY EDUCATION)*

	Technical		Cultural and other†		Together	
	1955	1966	1955	1966	1955	1966
Higher level	38·787	92·541	64·540	134·809	103·327	227·350
Secondary level	131·051	432·353	279·435	485·513	410·486	917·866
Together	169·838	524·894	343·975	620·322	513·813	1145·216

* In 1955 only in State; in 1966 in both State and co-operative sector. To the total must be added 1,700 (in 1955) and 2,700 (in 1966) persons self-employed but duly registered with their respective official and exclusive professional organisations, such as writers, scientific workers, architects, artists or composers.
† Including science, economy, planning and health service.

Source: CS *Statistical Yearbooks* (1967) pp. 113 and 116.

Less conspicuous, but nonetheless sociologically relevant, was the faster increase of specialists with technical training. In 1951/2 among those completing courses at higher secondary schools for vocational education there were 51·6 per cent who had studied in technical departments. In 1967/8 this share increased to 61·1 per cent. At the university level the share of those completing courses in technical studies increased from 37·1 per cent in 1951/2 to 47·8 per cent in 1967/8. The changes in the structure are reviewed in Table 23.

As can be seen from Table 23, the proportion of technical intelligentsia in the total of specialists with higher and secondary education increased from 33·1 per cent in 1955 to 45·8 per cent in 1966. The increase was more pronounced at the secondary level (from 31·9 to 47·1 per cent) than at the higher level (from 37·5 to 40·7 per cent). On the other hand, the higher/secondary level ratio remained, in the period observed, almost constant; specialists with higher education of both types made up about 20 per cent of the total in the year concerned.

The previously mentioned shift in the structure of the intelligentsia was not large enough to weaken the leading role of the cultural intelligentsia during the dramatic period of the late sixties. On the contrary, the technical intelligentsia found in many respects common ground with them and supported their endeavour for a general reform of the socialist system.

(c) AMOUNT OF INCOME

In Chapter 1(C) we have indicated, in the broadest possible outline, the impact of socialisation and income policy on the distribution of income by size. The narrowing of several important differentials has been shown and the magnitude of equalisation of income from all sources has been demonstrated by means of a Lorenz curve.

Now we shall deal with income distribution in more detail.

In order to get a series of data stretching over the longest possible period of time we shall first consider the income distribution of all wage and salary earners lumped together. In this way we can compare the recent development with the short postwar period of a mixed economy and also with the last prewar year (Table 24).

Table 24

INCOME FROM EMPLOYMENT BY SIZE
(INCOME RECIPIENTS—WORKERS AND OTHER EMPLOYEES TOGETHER)

Income before tax in thousand Kčs per year*			Percentage of income recipients				
1937	1947	1956–68	1937	1947	1959	1964	1968
-3	-24	0-7.2	27.2	27.17	1.69	0.32	0.09
3-6	24-30	7.2-9.6	28.8	16.37	6.39	2.85	1.04
6-9	30-36	9.6-12.0	18.1	15.22	13.37	10.02	4.76
9-12	36-42	12.0-14.4	9.8	11.26	16.98	15.56	9.74
12-15	42-48	14.4-16.8	7.9	8.33	16.68	15.96	13.26
	48-54	16.8-19.2		6.33	15.03	15.05	13.37
15-18	54-60	19.2-21.6	2.0	4.78	11.44	13.41	13.09
	Over 60	21.6-24.0		10.54	7.43	9.97	12.16
Over 18		24.0-30.0	6.2		7.84	11.78	19.34
		30.0-36.0			2.15	3.52	8.19
		36.0-42.0			0.64	1.04	2.93
		42.0-48.0			0.22	0.34	1.11
		Over 48.0			0.14	0.18	0.92
Total			100.0	100.0	100.0	100.0	100.0
Average yearly earning from employment in Kčs — nominal			11.568	39.899	15.888	17.472	21.000
Average yearly earning from employment in Kčs — real†			11.568	12.507	13.487	15.726	18.150

* Income brackets arranged according to the purchasing power equivalents. Conversion coefficients are 1947/1937 = 3.2; 1947/1959–68 = 2.5; Cost of living index (1937 = 100) 1947: 319; 1959: 117.8; 1964: 111.1; 1968: 115.7.
† In 1937 purchasing power.

Source: Data for 1937 and 1947 from Two Year Plan Report (Průběh plnění) pp. 316, 317, 344 and 352; for 1959 and 1964, 20 let, p. 181; for 1968, CS Statistical Yearbook (1969).

Although the purchasing power equivalents are not accurate, the income structure is fairly comparable. Table 24 reveals clearly the double movement; the increase of average real earnings and the narrowing of dispersion from this average. However, the uniform picture is attained only because the several odd years after the second monetary reform (1953) are omitted (from 1953 to 1955 the average real earnings dropped even below the prewar level), and some differentials which remained constant throughout this period are, in the global income distribution, more than offset by the equalisation in other respects. There might also be some doubts about the reliability of the cost of living index, which in comprising predominantly staple low-grade goods and services does not reflect the real consumer pattern in which items of greater price increase are more heavily represented. Nevertheless even with these reservations, which may lead to about a 10 per cent discount of the rate of growth, the picture is favourable enough, and were it not, as will be shown later on (Table 51), for a similarly or even more favourable development in countries which are usually classified as capitalist, the record of Czechoslovak income policy could be viewed with pride.

We shall return to the rate of growth in Chapter 3 (B). Concerning the levelling, it may be inferred from what was said earlier that it affected all types of incomes; however, this happened in a particular pattern, leaving some important differentials quite untouched. Whereas the gap between wage and salary decreased considerably, and similarly also the difference between the skilled and unskilled workers, and whereas within each of these categories the differences decreased, the male/female and active/retired earning ratios remained almost constant.

The gap between men's and women's income from employment was narrowed only slightly immediately after the war from 182 to 155, where women's average earnings equalled 100, and then remained almost constant. In 1963 the ratio was at 151.[1] Similarly in 1966.[2] The difference between men's and women's earnings remained constant in spite of a big relative

[1] Jiří Fremr, 'Rozdíly ve mzdách mužů a žen', in *Statistika* (1965) pp. 503 and ff.

[2] J. Večerník, in *Československá společnost*, p. 300.

increase in the women's qualification for work at all levels of training. The divergence of the respective dynamics is revealed in Table 25.

Table 25

FEMALE/MALE RATIOS IN QUALIFICATION AND EARNING
(FEMALE'S ACHIEVEMENT IN PER CENT OF MALE'S)

(Row 1–4: number of women per hundred men, row 5: per cent of men's earnings)

		1948	1953	1958	1963	1966	1969
1	Students of establishments for higher education	17·3	30·4	44·2	70·1	67·1	67·6
2	Students of secondary schools for vocational education*	80·3	90·7	74·1	94·6	103·2	122·9
3	Completed apprenticeship training	·	27·4†	29·7	38·7	51·5	47·4
4	Skilled personnel in industry, agriculture (state sector) and commerce‡	·	·	·	62·7[1]	71·6[2]	·
5	Average earning from employment	63·7[3]	·	·	66·2	66·0	·

* Including evening courses for employed people.
† 1955.
‡ Branches where in 1967 about a half of female labour force was employed. Data for other branches are lacking (with the exception of construction where the share of women employed is negligible).
[1] 1962.
[2] 1967.
[3] Weighted average of wage and salary excluding civil service and state enterprises, i.e. average for 80·8 per cent of labour force.

Sources: Row 1 to 4, CS *Statistical Yearbooks*; row 5, 1948, *Průběh plnění*, p. 330; 1963, J. Fremr, in *Statistika* (1965) p. 503; 1966, J. Večerník, in *Československá společnost*, p. 300.

Unfortunately, neither data on women's earnings nor data on the number of qualified women employed are disclosed regularly. We have to content ourselves with the scattered

and/or indirect indicators. However, they amply bear witness
to the fact that women's relative position within the income
distribution since 1946 not only did not improve but, in view of
a greater supply of qualified female labour force, deteriorated.

The second wide gap which the new income policy did not
diminish was the differential between active workers and
employees on one side and retired workers (pensioners) on the
other. In the immediate postwar period this difference somewhat increased but this was due to the sharp increase in the
number of income recipients. The ratio of the average pension
to the average earning was 32·3 per cent in 1937, and 28·1 per
cent in 1948; then it slightly improved, attaining 29·2 per cent
in 1958 and 30·2 per cent in 1968, without, however regaining
the prewar ratio.

A continuously growing share of population in the post-
productive age-group makes the prospect of the possible closing
of this gap still more unlikely. Until now the stress has been laid
on comprehensive coverage of old people with some income
rather than with bringing this income more in line with the
development of wages and salaries. Whereas the population
receiving some kind of pension or similar benefits increased
from 13·8 per cent in 1950 to 21·0 per cent of the whole population in 1968, the total amount of pensions and benefits in
relation to national income (in its official 'material' definition)
increased only from 6·2 to 7·4 per cent in the same period.[1]

On the other hand, it has to be taken into account that the
legal retiring age is fairly low – as a rule 60 years for men and
55 for women[2] – and that pensioners may, within certain limits,
take on part-time jobs without forfeiting their claims to the
full pension. As will be shown later on, these circumstances
play the most important role in the living standard of the
pensioners' households.

Otherwise, as regards the differentials of industry and type of

[1] Source: CS *Statistical Yearbooks*.

[2] With respect to women, the age of 55 is approximately the average, the
differing timing (from 53 to 56) depends on the number of children whom
the women in question have reared. Childless women are entitled to the full
pension only at 57. In the case of men the retiring age is reduced for those
who are working in extraordinarily difficult and/or unhealthy conditions
such as miners, radiologists, etc. Moreover, and significantly without much
publicity, policemen also are favoured in this way.

work, there were only a few exceptions from the general trend towards levelling. Looking at the three basic economic sectors (Table 26) a clear-cut convergence can be observed since before the war.

Table 26

EARNINGS DIFFERENTIALS BY ECONOMIC SECTORS
INCOME FROM EMPLOYMENT ONLY
(WAGES AND SALARIES TOGETHER)
IN PER CENT OF THE AVERAGE EARNING IN THE
WHOLE SOCIETY

	1935/6	1948	1953	1958	1963	1968
Primary production*	64·5	65·2	70·3	80·1	84·2	94·1
Secondary production†	132·7	110·4	109·4	106·7	106·5	104·3
Commercial services‡	87·2[1]	91·3	89·5	89·5	93·4	95·5

* Agriculture.
† Industry and construction.
‡ Transport, communication, commerce, catering, banking and insurance.
[1] Estimate on the basis of incomplete data.

Sources: Prewar and 1948, for earnings *Průběh plnění*, p. 336; for weights *Sborník o výstavbě ČSR* (Prague, 1946) p. 89, and CS *Statistical Yearbook* (1938) pp. 228 and 234; otherwise current CS *Statistical Yearbooks*.

Looking at individual industries (Table 27) we may observe a few shifts of considerable magnitude, shifts well characteristic of the new situation. The prewar top group among the workers' aristocracy (printing workers) definitely lost their leading position and are now scoring well below average. Similarly brewery workers (second among the workers' prewar aristocracy by wage rate). Unfortunately here we can only follow the development until 1948. Also the comparatively high average wage in the glass industry dropped considerably below the average. The leading position in the wage scale immediately after the war was taken over by the miners, who, however, even before the war, were among the top wage-earners (22 per cent above the average). The increase of their differential attained its apogee in 1960, since when it has decreased slightly.

Otherwise no conspicuous changes occurred. Surprisingly,

Table 27

WAGES DIFFERENTIALS BY SELECTED INDUSTRIES RANGED ACCORDING TO THE PREWAR RATIOS (IN PER CENT OF AVERAGE WAGE FOR THE TOTAL OF SECONDARY PRODUCTION IN THE YEARS CONCERNED)

1939 order		1939	1946	1948	1950	1955	1960	1965	1969	1969 order
I	Printing industry	143·2	103·2	99·1	87·4	90·9	90·2	88·6	93·5	IV
II	Breweries	132·5	107·5	103·2	.	.	.	.	.	.
III	Iron and steel industry	122·7*	.	.	126·4	125·2	122·7	121·8	118·1	II
IV	Mining	122·0	126·9	121·8	126·9	145·0	150·0	148·2	147·0	I
V	Construction	110·4	102·5	123·1	110·7	102·3	106·0	110·5	113·8	III
VI	Glass industry	107·2	94·2	91·4	88·0	90·0	87·8	86·3	89·8	V
VII	Clothing	79·7	90·7	87·0	77·9	70·2	71·5	73·3	75·9	VII
VIII	Textile industry	74·2	90·9	97·7	68·4	75·4	76·2	75·7	78·7	VI

Coverage and sources: 1939–48 hourly rates in Czech Lands only (their share in worked hours: 86 per cent in 1949); source: *Průběh plnění*, pp. 321 and 325. 1950–69 monthly earnings; source: CS *Statistical Yearbooks*.
* 1935, *Statistical Yearbook* (1941) p. 177.

construction and metallurgy, which are supposed to be favoured industries, have not attained a better range above average than before the war. Construction workers, after having enjoyed a considerable boom of private building activity in 1947 and 1948, had to accept, in spite of the expanding construction investment and scarce labour in the late fifties, a drop in their wages almost to the average. This might explain their often lamented lack of working morale and inclination to work for the private black market.

On the other hand, traditional textile and clothing industries staffed predominantly by women remain Cinderellas. The post-war boom for textile workers was a short-lived one. They suffered considerably under the continued impact of the second wave of nationalisation (commencing 1948) and preference for heavy industry. The first deprived them of the benefits of the private textile industry boom, the second of a favourable treatment by the planners – since 1950 all powerful. Similarly neglected branches might be found also within the food industry, but postwar data are not published in sufficient detail for that purpose. The food industry as a whole was continuously below average, however, improving its position somewhat from 89·8 per cent in 1955 to 95·4 per cent in 1968.

Turning to the income differentials by profession, we are still more embarrassed by the lack of data. Comparatively, the best information is provided for the secondary sector where average earnings of workers, technicians and administration personnel are regularly disclosed as separate items (Table 28).

Development of earning differentials by type of work in secondary production reveals two specific features. First, in dynamic perspective the stop, in the middle fifties, of the clear-cut levelling trend; then a period of mild oscillation, then, since about 1963, the prevalence of a slow anti-levelling tendency. (This resulted from the conscious reversal of the income policy.) Second, in the cross-section view, a tendency can be observed towards increasing mainly the earning ratio of technical personnel, and on the other hand, keeping salaries of administrative personnel below the level of workers' wages. This ranging was achieved by the income policy in the early fifties. Wage regulations in the wake of the second monetary reform in June 1953 brought about the culmination of this development.

Table 28

EARNING DIFFERENTIALS BY TYPE OF WORK IN THE SECONDARY PRODUCTION

(AVERAGES IN PER CENT OF WORKER'S WAGE)

	1948	1950	1953	1955	1958	1960	1963	1965	1966	1967	1968	1969
(a) Industry												
Technical Personnel	148·6	·	129·4	125·3	131·6	132·9	126·7	135·3	140·5	142·3	140·9	142·9
Administrative Personnel	148·6	·	88·2	85·0	88·1	87·1	83·7	86·3	88·6	90·2	89·3	92·0
(b) Construction												
Technical Personnel	177·2	150·4	127·2	125·3	125·3	131·3	121·3	129·0	132·0	134·8	135·2	135·0
Administrative Personnel	126·9	107·8	89·3	84·7	83·9	87·5	81·3	80·6	83·9	85·8	85·1	82·7

Source: CS *Statistical Yearbook* (1970); for industry in 1948, *Průběh plnění*, p. 343.

However, after 1963 administrative personnel in industry (not in construction) were also allowed to slightly improve their earning ratio.

Outside secondary production there are only scattered data on the amount of income.[1] Nevertheless their compilation and, possibly comparison with some professions in industry (Table 29), supply enough evidence on the fact that the differentials between white- and blue-collar workers ceased to play an important role and that it is individual vocations – conceived as narrowly as possible – which matter.

Within these the differentials are sometimes most surprising for the outside observer. The leading position of the managers and miners might be well understood, but a higher reward for a turner's than a doctor's work and the higher earning of a dairywoman than of a babies' nurse (whose earning in 1965 was less than a half of the former) bear witness to a particularly production-orientated hierarchy of values. On the other hand, it has to be added that criticism of these and similar disparities could be heard since the early sixties even from official sources[2] and that after 1965 salaries of specialists with higher, especially university education, increased more than the overall average, though without fully eliminating the former disparities.

According to sociological research, the scope and results of which will be discussed later on, in 1967 almost 70 per cent of employees in the highest income bracket (that with over 2,500 Kčs net of taxes per month) had less than a high-level education. Almost a third in that bracket did not even attain the lower secondary level of education. (Table 30.)

Unfortunately no data have been disclosed on the earnings in the ruling apparats. Numbers and salaries of the armed forces and of the Party officials are not included in the labour and wage statistics and information of both has always been regarded as a State secret. However, those who have lived in a Communist State know all too well that salaries of these groups, especially

---

[1] Data on average earnings in administration, education, health, science, and research are not very revealing. Lumping together highly qualified with unskilled auxiliary personnel, they are moving either around or slightly below the overall average.

[2] Most of the information in Table 29 is due to such a critical evaluation published in the official Communist Party daily.

Table 29

EARNINGS IN SELECTED PROFESSIONS IN 1965

Profession	Average monthly earnings in Kčs	Index (in per cent of average in the society)
Leading manager in engineering industry	4692*	314
Coal-face miner (skilled)	3521†	236
Chief doctor of a regional hospital	3381‡	226
Scientific worker (graduate)	3022†	202
Lathe operator (8th wage class)	2422†	162
Locomotive driver	2363‡	158
Doctor-practitioner (with wide experience)	2243†	150
Foreman in heavy engineering	2149‡	144
Locksmith (6th wage class)	2010†	135
Lawyer (graduate)	1937[1]	130
Grammar school teacher (graduate)	1907†	128
Bricklayer	1865‡	125
Labourer (5th wage class)	1757†	118
Dairywoman	1632†	109
Elementary school teacher	1288†	86
Hospital nurse	1178†	79
Shop assistant	1011‡	68
Charwoman	940[1]	63
Nursery nurse (schooled)	802†	54
Average of the total labour force	1493[2]	100

* *Sociologický časopis*, V (1969), no. 6, p. 610; salary computed for 1965 from the percentage ratio to the average wage in engineering in 1967.
† *Rudé Právo*, 14 March 1967.
‡ Jan Průša, *Ekonomické řízení a mzdové soustavy* (Prague, 1969) p. 91.
[1] *Statistika* (1965), no. 11 (data for October 1963).
[2] CS *Statistical Yearbooks*.

of army and security officers, range farther to the top, sur-
passing as a rule the average earnings of miners.

Table 30

HIGHEST EARNINGS STRUCTURE BY LEVEL OF EDUCATION
(IN PER CENT OF RECIPIENTS OF 2500 KČS AND MORE,
NET OF TAXES PER MONTH)

With higher education	30·8
With upper secondary education	26·4
With lower secondary education	10·7
With apprenticeship training	16·7
With completed elementary education	9.5
With uncompleted elementary education	5·9

Source: J. Večerník, in *Československá společnost*, p. 306.

On the other hand, there are also members of the cultural
intelligentsia who may attain a very high income and even
appear at the top of the scale at large. Writers and artistes and,
in a way, architects also, being able to work to the special orders
of different bodies, have fared much better than the other
professions. Those of them who were willing to satisfy the
Party's orders, not hesitating to follow its changing line, could –
by supplying the means of education (especially the mass
media) with regular staff – achieve extraordinary incomes,
exceeding 10,000 or even 20,000 Kčs per month, equivalent to
approximately £3–6,000 per annum. Similarly, popular artistes
insofar as they did not infringe the ideological barrier could
earn more money than the former aristocracy of the intelligentsia – doctors and lawyers, who now being either civil servants
or enterprise employees could reasonably heighten their income
only if doing an additional part-time job, to which of course
there are not only certain legal but also physical limits.

In general, it may be concluded that, with the exception of
1968 and the period immediately before, it was collaboration on
the cultural plane which could bring in the greatest legal amount
of income.

All this is significant to what has already been said on the
changes in the occupational pattern in Chapter 2 (B) and still

has to be said on the new pattern of power in Chapter 2 (F).

Individual income however, does not reflect the true position
which is precondition of living standard. Fortunately, there are,
on the basis of sample investigations of family accounts and on
the basis of microcensuses covering one representative per cent
of households, sufficient data on family income and expenditure
by social groups (workers, employees, co-operative farmers and
sometimes also pensioner households). Using the most amply
published data from the microcensus investigating income and
expenditure in 1965, and examining at first all households
together, we get the overall picture in Table 31.

Comparatively very small average households and a high
percentage of gainfully employed women (and partially of
other family members) are two factors which are improving the
income/expenditure level of Czechoslovak households. It may
be inferred that, up to an average income per head of about
15,000 Kčs per year, the other family members' gainful occupations are a substantial contribution to the rise of income.

In 1965 81 per cent of households, with a membership
totalling 84 per cent of the population, had a per capita net
money income below 12,000 Kčs which is the equivalent of
about £625 per year.[1] Including income in kind this percentage might drop to 75 per cent or 80 per cent respectively;
24 per cent of households (with 25 per cent of population) had a
per capita net income below a half of this sum (equivalent of
about £312 per year). Including income in kind this poverty
group might be reduced to less than 20 per cent.

In individual socio-economic groups (Table 32) the share of
the poor stratum below the equivalent of £312 per year,
including income in kind, would be: in workers' households
13–15 per cent, in the employees' households around 6 per cent,
in the households of co-operative farmers about 12 per cent and
in households of pensioners 30 per cent.

The position of average per capita income (including income
in kind) was in individual social groups in relation to the overall
average of income as follows: in workers' families 98·6 per cent,

---

[1] This is the purchasing power equivalent, the assessment of which is
discussed in Jaroslav Krejčí, 'Gross National Product in the United King-
dom and Czechoslovakia', in *Soviet Studies*, XXII (1971) pp. 370–1.

Income brackets† (Kčs)	Number of households	Average number of members	Of which economically active	Money income net of taxes per head (Kčs)	Income in kind per head (Kčs)
–2,400	749	2·59	0·40	1,631	816
2,401–3,600	1,296	2·80	0·41	3,127	706
3,601–4,800	2,996	3·55	0·65	4,301	632
4,801–6,000	4,525	3·58	0·89	5,412	613
6,001–7,200	5,132	3·57	1·18	6,602	561
7,201–8,400	5,108	3·60	1·50	7,804	530
8,401–9,600	4,799	3·48	1·70	8,980	461
9,601–10,800	4,052	3·29	1·84	10,164	426
10,801–12,000	3,139	3·06	1·91	11,374	398
12,001–13,200	2,306	2·88	2·01	12,562	383
13,201–14,400	1,693	2·55	1·98	13,759	376
14,401–15,600	1,194	2·47	2·06	14,958	426
15,601–16,800	831	2·22	1·95	16,155	307
16,801–18,000	562	2·08	1·87	17,364	368
18,001–19,200	341	1·93	1·74	18,503	245
19,201–20,400	188	1·90	1·71	19,748	405
20,401–21,600	107	1·74	1·51	21,001	214
21,601–22,800	78	1·55	1·42	22,149	274
22,801–24,000	57	1·58	1·32	23,433	492
24,001 and more	122	1·55	1·32	28,596	463
Total	39,275	3·24	1·44	8,467	510

* I.e. workers', other employees', co-operative farmers' and pensioners' households.
† Money income net of taxes per head and year.

Source: CS *Statistical Yearbook*, 1967 (microcensus in March 1966).

Table 32

HOUSEHOLDS' PER CAPITA INCOME BY SIZE, SOURCE AND SOCIAL GROUP IN 1965

Money income brackets* (in Kčs)	Workers' households		Employees' households		Co-operative farmers' households		Pensioners' households		All households	
	Number	Per cent	Number	Per cent	Number	Per cent	Number	Per cent	Number	Per cent
-6,000	2,655	17·7	616	7·2	787	24·9	4,553	45·9	9,566	24·3
6,001–12,000	9,171	61·0	5,181	60·5	1,815	57·3	4,713	47·6	22,230	56·6
12,001–18,000	2,878	19·1	2,350	27·5	502	15·8	604	6·1	6,586	16·8
18,001 and more	335	2·2	414	4·8	65	2·0	41	0·4	893	2·3
Total	15,039	100·0	8,561	100·0	3,169	100·0	9,911	100·0	39,275†	100·0
	Amount of income		*Amount of income*		*Amount of income*		*Amount of income*		*Amount of income*	
	In Kčs	Per cent	In Kčs	Per cent	In Kčs	Per cent	In Kčs	Per cent	In Kčs	Per cent
Average money income per head a year	8,479	100·0	10,013	100·0	8,118	100·0	6,993	100·0	8,467	100·0
Of which from employment	7,162	84·5	8,798	87·9	1,415	17·4	1,779	25·4	5,953	70·3
From agriculture	53	0·6	25	0·3	5,516	67·9	379	5·4	697	8·2
From national insurance	1,172	13·8	1,080	10·7	1,086	13·4	4,691	67·1	1,664	19·7
From other sources	92	1·1	110	1·1	101	1·3	144	2·1	153	1·8
To which added income in kind	369	4·4	191	1·9	1,512	18·6	462	6·6	510	6·0

* Income net of taxes per head and year.
† The difference between this item and the sum of households in the individual social groups is unaccounted for.

in employees' families 113·7 per cent, in co-operative farmers' families 107·3 per cent and in pensioners' households 83 per cent. This is not a great discrepancy.

It is surprising that the co-operative farmers rank well before the workers and that the pensioners on average are much better off than their poverty ratio (more than double of that of workers') indicates. However, all this is due to the fact that neither co-operative farmers nor retired persons live only from that source of income which characterises their socio-economic group. As can be seen from Table 32, the income from agriculture constituted in 1965 only 68 per cent of farmers' families' income, and income from social insurance only 67 per cent of that of pensioners' households. In the case of co-operative farmers the ratio of income from other sources than agriculture was in individual income brackets almost the same and rather declining towards the higher brackets, forming less than 8 per cent in the income group with more than 24,000 Kčs per year per head. In the pensioners' households the income from other sources other than social insurance increased with income (from 8 per cent at the bottom to 55 per cent at the top), i.e. this other income was the main source of a satisfactory living standard in pensioners' households. Pensioners' households which were more than 80 per cent dependent on social insurance were among those 30 per cent with per capita income less than £312 per annum.

A dynamic picture can be obtained only for the basic three groups, i.e. excluding pensioners (Table 33), and with respect to other years than the review mentioned before.[1] Nevertheless the figures might be accepted as fairly reflecting at least the basic trends of development.

Household finances viewed from the side of expenditure and calculated at constant prices (Table 34) reveal some surprising features.

In 1955 average per capita money income in a worker's family was only slightly lower than that of an employee's family. If income in kind were to be added the difference might

[1] For the methodological and technical difficulties in comparing the sample results with those of microcensuses see Josef Vytlačil, 'Některé metodické problémy statistiky rodinných účtů', in *Statistika* (1970) pp. 393 and ff.

disappear. On the other hand the per capita money income in a
co-operative farmer's family was substantially lower and would
remain so even with the addition of income in kind. However,
since then both employees' and co-operative farmers' income
has developed much more favourably than that of workers.
This is a strange phenomenon in a 'dictatorship of the proletariat', but as has been demonstrated earlier the workers'
relative position (most attributes of their status) within the

Table 33

INCOME DISTRIBUTION BY SIZE AND SOCIAL GROUPS
IN 1956 AND 1967

Per capita money income in Kčs per year	Percentage of households					
	Workers		Employees		Co-operative farmers	
	1956	1967	1956	1967	1956	1967
−2,400	1·7	0·1	0·3	0·1	15·9	0·3
2,400–4,800	28·8	5·4	21·9	1·3	36·8	6·0
4,800–7,200	33·7	21·0	34·8	9·2	25·6	19·3
7,200–9,600	20·0	25·9	23·1	19·5	13·2	23·8
9,600–12,000	10·3	21·0	11·1	24·6	4·8	20·9
12,000–14,400	4·0	13·2	5·5	19·6	2·6	11·9
14,400–16,800	1·0	7·7	2·1	12·1	0·6	9·4
16,800–19,200	0·3	3·5	0·8	7·4	0·3	4·2
Over 19,200	0·2	2·2	0·4	6·2	0·2	4·2

Data from microcensuses, source: 25 let, p. 194.

society improved already so much that the political leadership
found it expedient to reverse the trend. Now, the main stress
was on the higher rate of growth for qualified cadres – the
managers and apparatchiks of course included.

On the other hand the flight from agriculture especially of the
younger generation,[1] at a rate not compensated for by the

[1] In 1930 13·3 per cent of persons working in agriculture were below
twenty. In 1956 the proportion of this age group dropped to 7·8 and in 1965
to 4·3 per cent only. From 1960 propaganda campaigns were launched to

application of modern technology, induced the planners to a more favourable price policy for the farmers. Even without that, however, farmers would be able to improve their relative position as a result of two developments: growing output and decreasing number of persons employed.[1] Nevertheless it is

Table 34

HOUSEHOLDS' MONEY EXPENDITURE DIFFERENTIALS
(IN 1955 PRICES; WORKERS' HOUSEHOLDS MONEY
EXPENDITURE EQUALS 100)

	1955	1960	1965	1969
Employees	103·7	108·5	113·3	119·8
Co-operative farmers	77·0	74·1	90·9	99·8

Source: 25 let, p. 197.

surprising that the co-operative farmers have improved their position so much that their average per capita money income equals that in a worker's family; with income in kind included, this puts the co-operative farmers into a much better position than that of the workers already in 1965. This might be partly due to the fact that according to the same microcensus there were in a farmer's household 1·92 persons gainfully employed whereas in a worker's family only 1·76.

The fact that in agriculture as a whole the average age of working population was about eight years higher than in other branches of the economy[2] and for this reason the earnings might be higher, was outweighed by the higher proportion of women (51 against 45 per cent in the average) which operates in the opposite direction.

There seems to be no particular bias in the microcensus'

---

attract young people to agriculture. However, of 160,000 persons gained in such a way in the period 1961–5 only 51,000 were still working in agriculture at the close of that period. For details see Jiří Karlík *et al. Československé zemědělství a pracovní síly* (Prague, 1967) pp. 40–1.

[1] Since 1960 even the co-operative sector, the personnel of which until then was growing because of the collectivisation in progress, has declined in population.

[2] Jiří Karlík *et al. Československé zemědělství*, p. 45.

comparatively high income of co-operative farmers. According
to the comprehensive agricultural statistics the amount of
monetary compensation for co-operative farmers totalled, in
1965, 8·165 million Kčs; this gives 6,703 Kčs per head per year,
i.e. 21·5 per cent more than the microcensus' equivalent
(5,516 Kčs). On the other hand, the annual average worker's
wage in industry (data for the whole economy put together
workers' wages and employees' salaries) was in the same year,
according to the industrial statistics, 18·348 Kčs. Recalculated
on a per capita basis in an average worker's household with
3·69 members of which 1·76 gainfully employed, it totals
8,751 Kčs per head and year, i.e. 22·2 per cent higher than the
microcensus' equivalent (7,162 Kčs).

Also the magnitude of the growing disparity between employees' and workers' families per capita income seems to be
consistent with what has been ascertained in respect to the
relative growth of wages and salaries in secondary production
(see Table 28).

A development similar to that of average per capita income
can be realised in following the structure of income distribution
(Table 33). In 1956 there was in this respect a similarity between
workers' and employees' families. On the other hand the
co-operative farmers with more than a half of households in the
lowest brackets lagged far behind. In 1967 the employees'
household shifted more impressively to higher brackets than
workers' households; the new income pattern of the latter,
however, was almost echoed by that of co-operative farmers.

Unfortunately this cannot be taken as a corroboration of the
earlier analysis. Derived from the same basic data the structure
of income distribution cannot but reflect the same trend as the
average data.

(D) CONSUMPTION, WEALTH AND STYLE OF LIFE

Although income is incontestably the necessary precondition
of living standard, the latter can be, within the same amount of
income, differently shaped according to consumer preferences;
these in their turn are mainly influenced by the type of education and by the actual occupation.

In the preceding chapter we have stated a narrow margin

between the average income of workers', employees' and co-operative farmers' families, and also a similar pattern of their income distribution. Naturally this is reflected also in the consumption.

Table 35

EXPENDITURE PATTERN BY SOCIAL GROUPS
INCLUDING CONSUMPTION IN KIND
(PERCENTAGE IN CURRENT PRICES)

	Workers			Employees			Co-operative farmers		
	1955	1965	1968	1955	1965	1968	1955	1965	1968
Food	51·5	40·9	36·6	49·3	37·2	32·1	47·6	41·4	36·2
Industrial goods	21·9	23·9	26·4	21·2	24·2	27·3	24·1	26·3	30·8
Services	11·1	11·3	11·2	13·0	13·9	13·6	7·6	9·0	9·4
Other*	15·5	23·9	25·8	16·5	24·7	27·0	20·7	23·3	23·6

* Direct taxes, savings, lending and expenditure on husbandry.

Source: 25 let, p. 199, and CS *Statistical Yearbook* (1967).

Considering the broad lines of household expenditure, there were in 1955 no considerable differences in expenditure by social groups. In 1968 they were still narrower. However, a surprising fact is the low proportion of expenditure on services which is due to two circumstances: low prices and inadequate supply of most services. This is especially the case with housing, but also with laundries, maintenance, repair workshops, etc. The exceptionally low level of rent has been already mentioned (page 23); other aspects of housing will be dealt with shortly. The low proportion of expenditure on services is also partly due to the fact that the rental value of owner-occupied houses, which plays an important role especially in farmers' households, is not included.

As far as consumption by social groups in physical units is concerned, only data for basic food in workers' and employees' families in Czech Lands are available (Table 36).

Table 36

AVERAGE CONSUMPTION OF BASIC FOODS IN WORKERS' AND EMPLOYEES' HOUSEHOLDS
(CZECH LANDS ONLY; IN KG PER HEAD AND YEAR)

	1931/2	1948	1950	1953	1955	1960	1965	1969
					Workers' Households			
Meat and products of meat	33·81	30·80	38·77	33·35	37·40	40·44	43·15	49·54
Fats	16·63	13·12	16·24	15·35	17·89	17·84	18·40	18·48
Of which butter	3·19	3·14	5·99	4·92	6·21	7·80	8·27	8·51
Milk (litres)	130·20	144·40	156·18	137·45	133·56	115·53	116·01	112·45
Eggs (pieces)	142	117	177	130	149	183	202	217
Bread	71·43	91·05	76·27	69·99	67·92	68·42	66·46	62·06
Sugar	24·20	17·50	20·15	17·96	22·29	20·15	19·25	19·17
					Employees' Households			
Meat and products of meat	47·47	29·74	37·45	31·22	36·75	37·50	39·31	44·86
Fats	17·32	13·24	16·44	15·56	17·52	16·57	17·08	16·90
Of which butter	7·03	3·87	6·40	5·79	7·03	8·20	8·73	8·81
Milk (litres)	152·99	142·30	151·89	137·29	140·45	119·24	111·97	107·62
Eggs (pieces)	219	142	196	145	159	172	196	205
Bread	52·48	74·34	67·10	63·22	62·65	62·10	56·54	52·35
Sugar	22·61	17·81	21·03	18·27	21·98	18·42	17·69	17·40

Source: 25 let, p. 201.

These figures are significant in two aspects. First they indicate that the food consumption pattern in workers' and employees' families became similar during the war; after that the consumption of staple food increased more in workers' families. Whereas the former converging development was apparently a result of rationing and full employment in the years of war – in the latter differentiation the workers' preference for staple food rather than a more variegated diet can be seen; the only item in which employees' consumption, still in 1968, exceeded that of the workers was butter.

Second, data in Table 36 corroborate our statement on the decrease of real incomes as a result of the monetary reform in 1953 (see p. 64). They also help to assess the probable intensity of the drop below the prewar level which was particularly conspicuous with respect to the employees' households.[1]

Within the field of industrial goods, the proportions of expenditure on clothing, which is one of the main items in this group, seem to have converged throughout the whole period. In 1955 it constituted 36·8 per cent in workers' households, 34·4 per cent in those of employees and 39·1 per cent in those of co-operative farmers. In 1968 the percentages were 30·3, 28·5 and 28·9 respectively.

On the basis of further investigation we realise that the expenditure on basic consumer goods differs with respect to the amount of income and to the size of the family, rather than with respect to social groups. Expenditure on food in workers' families varied according to the amount of income – from 52·6 at the bottom to 29·7 per cent at the top in 1966; according to the number of children – from 41·5 (with one child) to 49·0 per cent (with six or more children) if the mother is at home, when she is employed from 31·3 to 45·2 per cent.

The situation was similar in the employees' households and also with respect to other items of consumer expenditure. This has been corroborated by the most recent, 1969 data, which are reproduced in Table 37.

Differences among social groups *qua* groups can be ascer-

---

[1] Global per capita data, reproduced in *Hospodářský a společenský vývoj Československa* (Prague, 1968), p. 128, do not indicate such a conspicuous decline in 1953. However, they may suffer more from inaccuracies due to the fact that prewar statistics are less comprehensive. Prewar and postwar

Table 37

MONEY EXPENDITURE BY HOUSEHOLDS IN 1969

	Workers with net money income per head and year in Kčs				Employees with net money income per head and year in Kčs			
	Together	Below 7,200	7,201–12,000	12,001 and more	Together	Below 7,200	7,201–12,000	12,001 and more
Food	33·9	45·2	36·5	29·9	29·5	42·3	34·9	26·4
Industrial goods	27·5	26·2	27·0	28·0	28·6	25·5	27·5	29·3
Services	11·3	9·0	11·2	11·8	13·9	13·2	13·3	14·1
Taxes and social insurance	17·5	14·0	16·5	19·1	17·9	13·2	16·3	18·8
Savings	8·5	4·9	7·6	9·9	9·1	4·8	7·1	10·3
Other expenditure	1·3	0·7	1·2	1·3	1·0	1·0	0·9	1·1

Source: CS *Statistical Yearbook* (1970) p. 457.

tained mainly with respect to other phenomena; (*a*) with respect to housing conditions and associated consumer durables and (*b*) with respect to the utilisation of leisure, especially consumption of cultural values.

Housing conditions are an element of wealth rather than of income distribution. This is especially valid in Czechoslovakia, where the majority of population lives in houses built before the war (according to the 1961 census, 77 per cent dwelling houses were built before 1945),[1] where the majority of the population live in private family houses (almost 70 per cent in 1961, agricultural homesteads included)[2] and where rent is so low that it cannot operate as a market lever and new flats are widely allotted rather than obtained for money. Thus the possession of a flat is rather an independent element of status.

Also in respect of apartment houses there is little amount of fluctuation because owners have virtually no right to give notice to the tenant and those who possess a good flat prefer to travel a long distance to work than move. There is a higher job fluctuation than migration within the area, where the jobs are still accessible. On the other hand the applicants for new flats have to spend years on the waiting list, or since the beginning of the sixties have to save a considerable sum of money and possibly work many hours on the 'brigades' in order to provide a co-operative flat. Construction of private houses, of course only family not apartment houses, is also possible; surprisingly, however, family houses are not – for reasons which will be explained shortly – indicative of higher status.

The proportion of different categories of flat acquisition may be deduced from Table 38, showing the development of newly constructed flats by type of ownership.

Whereas in 1960, over 60 per cent of new flats (rows 2 and 3 in Table 38) were allotted according to the waiting lists and possibly according to the social conditions of the claimants, in 1965 this proportion had dropped to 26 per cent; it then in-

representative data referring to social groups seem to be more comparable in coverage.

[1] Alois Andrle, Miroslav Pojer and Ota Ullmann, *Byty a bydlení v Československu* (Prague, 1967) p. 27.

[2] Ibid. p. 21.

creased again, however, to about 34 per cent in 1970. Private
family houses, the proportion of which constituted about a
quarter of new housing during the sixties, were built predominantly in rural areas, located mainly in Slovakia where
the shortage of housing was the greatest and the labour cost the
lowest.

Table 38

NEWLY CONSTRUCTED FLATS BY TYPE OF OWNERSHIP

		1948	*1950*	*1955*	*1960*	*1965*	*1970*
1	Number of newly com- pleted flats	21,683	38,238	48,790	73,766	77,818	112,135
	Of which per cent						
2	State owned buildings	54·8	76·2	69·3	57·1	25·8	16·8
3	Enterprise buildings*	—	—	—	6·6	0·3	17·6
4	Housing co- operatives' buildings	—	—	—	12·0	49·2	39·4
5	Private (family) houses	45·2	23·8	30·7	24·3	24·7	26·2

* Including farmers' co-operatives.

Source: 25 let, p. 212; CS *Statistical Yearbook* (1971) p. 218.

From 1955 to 1964 more than a half of private family houses
were built in Slovakia; of the total more than four-fifths were
built (in the years 1961–4) in localities with less than 5,000
population, and about two-thirds were inhabited by workers'
families.[1] Expensive family houses in suburbs of large towns
were mostly built before the war and are now often divided into
several flats, inhabited by different families. Under these
conditions there is no surprise in the discovery made by sociological research in 1967, which found that the ownership of a

[1] *Byty a bydlení v Československu*, pp. 149–51.

family house is not a function of higher income but on the contrary is usually connected with the lower income brackets.[1]

Bearing this in mind we might proceed to the investigation of the scale of housing conditions which were most completely assessed by the census in 1961. In breakdown by social groups, the structure of housing by size and quality is reviewed in Table 39.

Table 39

HOUSING PATTERN BY SOCIAL GROUPS IN 1961
(IN PER CENT OF HOUSEHOLDS IN EACH GROUP)

	Households			
(*a*) By size of flats Number of rooms (including kitchen) per flat (apartment)	*Workers*	*Employees*	*Co-operative farmers*	*Pensioners*
5 and more	4·2	8·3	5·0	3·8
4	12·5	22·4	13·7	8·9
3	38·5	42·5	42·2	26·0
2	38·5	21·9	35·1	46·1
1	6·3	4·9	4·0	15·2
(*b*) By quality of flats				
1 Flats with central heating	7·0	20·3	0·2	2·7
2 Flats without central heating but with all other accessories	15·0	33·3	1·9	11·8
3 Flats without central heating but with partial accessories	14·6	15·7	12·5	12·2
4 Flats without central heating or any accessories	63·4	30·7	85·4	73·3

Source: *Sčítání lidu domů a bytů v ČSSR*, vol. III, ed. UKLS (Prague, 1965).

Here the difference between individual social groups is much more conspicuous than was the case with the income and consumer expenditure patterns. Both the wealth indicators, that of

[1] J. Večerník, in *Československá společnost*, p. 315.

size and that of quality of flat, reveal a much higher living standard of employees than of the other social groups. The position of the other groups, however, is different, with respect to the size: the co-operative farmers are second and the pensioners are at the bottom; with respect to the quality of the flats the workers are second and the farmers are at the bottom. In general it may be inferred that the comparatively high material consumption of peasants is more than matched by their inferior dwellings.

This is only partly due to the old disparity between town and village. Better houses in many villages indicate a non-agricultural vocation of their holders. The Czech, and increasingly also Slovak villages, is an economically very mixed settlement. As can be seen from Table 40, only villages with less than 300 population were, in 1950, predominantly agricultural localities.

Table 40

RURAL POPULATION BY OCCUPATION IN 1950
(IN PER CENT OF THE TOTAL IN THE RESPECTIVE BRACKET)

Settlements with population	Agriculture	Industry	Other
−100	70·7	13·0	16·3
100–200	59·8	17·5	22·7
200–300	52·4	21·4	26·2
300–500	46·4	24·6	29·0
500–1,000	37·5	29·7	32·8

Source: Bohuslav Šedivý-Miroslav Zubina, 'Drobní držitelé půdy a jejich úloha v našem hospodárství', in *Nová mysl*, XIV (1960) p. 79.

Although it is possible to obtain a fairly good house in the countryside, cities provide housing conditions with a superior infrastructure both in technological and social respects. Therefore there is a continuous tendency – especially attractive for young people – to move to the cities.

In wanting to assess this movement in quantitative terms, we have to bear in mind that there is not only a move from the countryside to the cities and a growth of larger individual settlements but also a continuing amalgamation of civil parishes (boroughs and communes), and that the statistics reflect sometimes indiscriminately both these movements. Nevertheless, following separately the changes in the numbers of communes and in the number of population living in different groups by size, we may obtain a comparatively fair picture of both these shifts (Table 41).

Table 41

STRUCTURE OF LOCALITIES BY SIZE
(IN PER CENT OF THE RESPECTIVE TOTALS)

Bracket (group by number of inhabitants)		*Civil parishes*			*Population*			
		1950	*1961*	*1970*	*1930*	*1950*	*1961*	*1970*
to	199	30·2	18·7	16·2	2·4	4·5	2·3	1·7
200 to	499	36·5	35·8	34·5	14·8	14·1	10·3	8·6
500 to	999	19·1	24·2	25·9	18·1	15·8	14·8	13·5
1,000 to	1,999	8·8	12·6	13·6	16·9	14·3	15·1	13·8
2,000 to	4,999	3·9	6·3	6·8	17·7	14·2	16·4	15·0
5,000 to	9,999	0·9	1·4	1·6	7·5	7·4	8·6	8·3
10,000 to	19,999	0·4	0·6	0·8	6·1	6·1	7·2	8·0
20,000 to 49,999		0·2	0·3	0·4	5·6	6·7	7·2	8·8
50,000 to 99,999		—	0·1	0·1	0·9	2·9	4·0	6·5
100,000 or more		—	—	0·1	10·0	14·0	14·1	15·8

Source: *Byty a bydlení v ČS*, p. 215 and CS *Statistical Yearbooks*, 1938 and 1971.

Whereas in 1930 slightly more than a half and in 1950 almost a half of the Czechoslovak population lived in communes with less than 2,000 inhabitants, in 1970 this proportion had dropped to 38 per cent. The size bracket which gained most were the cities with 50,000 to 100,000 population. Their proportion increased from 1 per cent in 1930 to above 6 per cent of total population in 1970. Cities with over 100,000 increased their population by about half; their population increased from 10 to more than 15 per cent of the total. Otherwise, however, no conspicuous changes occurred.

In general it should be realised that the move from rural to urban areas was slower than the shift from agriculture to other employment. This trend can be followed already since 1921. From then to 1961 the agricultural population declined by

47·3 per cent, whereas the rural population by 21 per cent only. Between 1950 and 1961 the decline was 14 and 3 per cent respectively.[1]

The migrations mentioned apparently reflect, among other things, a shift towards better living conditions. A great deal in this respect has been achieved by the colonisation of the former German territories. Nevertheless, the housing space in the frontier areas was not fully utilised, and on the other hand did not alleviate the shortage of flats in the big cities in the other parts of the country. The shortage became especially acute as a result of low rents and increasing income. An inadequate flat is still considered as one of the main reasons for legal abortion.[2]

Despite all the publicity, the construction of new flats seems to have remained below prewar level during most of the post-war period (see Table 42). Although the prewar data refer to conurbations with more than 10,000 population only they are available for comparison with postwar data. The link may be provided by the nation-wide statistics of flats in new buildings authorised for use by permit; these data were published in years 1947–9 and corresponding figures for 1937 were officially reconstructed. Their mutual comparison indicates a still greater drop in building activity between 1937 and 1947–9 than is reflected by the data with different coverage. According to the latter the net yearly increase of flats was 4·0 per 1,000 population during the twenty-two postwar years (1948–69), whereas during the sixteen prewar years (1922–37) the ratio was 6·6 per year. Only in two lean years (1922 and 1935) was the prewar ratio lower than the postwar average.

This evaluation is corroborated by the 1961 census data on the pattern of living houses by age. Of the total number of flats which were then in use, 33·4 per cent were built in the period 1920–45, and 19·7 per cent between 1946 and 1961.[3] Converted

---

[1] Jiří Karlík et al. *Československé zemědělství*, p. 91.

[2] Abortions became legalised and supervised by the Ministry of Health in 1958. In that year the number of legally performed abortions made 37·5 per cent of live births. In the following ten years the yearly average ratio was 50·7 per cent. During all the eleven years together the abortions were in 82·2 per cent motivated by social and only in 17·8 per cent by health reasons. For details see Karel Vácha, 'Důsledky zákona o umělém přerušení těhotenství', in *Demografie*, XII (1970) pp. 48 and ff.

[3] *Byty a bydlení v Československu*, p. 23.

Table 42

ANNUAL NET INCREASE OF FLATS PER 1,000 POPULATION

	In 70 larger conurbations	Throughout the country	
		In buildings authorised for use by a permit	In all buildings
1922	3·2		
1923	4·4		
1924	6·2		
1925	5·0		
1926	5·7		
1927	8·2		
1928	12·3		
1929	9·0		
1930	7·7		
1931	9·6		
1932	10·3		
1933	5·1		
1934	4·0		
1935	3·3		
1936	5·4		
1937	5·7	2·9	
1947		0·2	
1948		0·5	1·8
1949		0·8	2·4
1950			3·1
1951			2·5
1952			3·1
1953			3·0
1954			2·9
1955			3·6
1956			4·5
1957			4·2
1958			3·4
1959			4·4
1960			4·7
1961			5·5
1962			5·7
1963			5·5
1964			4·9
1965			4·4
1966			3·6
1967			4·6
1968			5·0
1969			5·0
1970			6·0

Source: First column, *Statistical Yearbook* (1941); Second column, *Statistical Bulletin* (1950); third column, postwar CS *Statistical Yearbooks*.

to the per annum basis, and excluding the war years, when the negligible amount of new construction was far outnumbered by destructions, we get the following ratios: 1·67 for the prewar period, and 1·31 for the postwar period. The difference here is understandably smaller than that given by construction statistics, because – as said earlier – the whole housing space in frontier areas was not resettled and hence the number of flats which were in use in 1961 is smaller than the number of flats which were being constructed before this date, especially before 1946, when the transfer of Germans was undertaken.

Another aspect of housing conditions is the furniture, among which especially some modern electrical devices such as washing machines, refrigerators, vacuum cleaners, television sets, etc., are supposed to be indicators of the social status of their owners. In a country where, as a rule, only means of consumption are legally the objects of private ownership, these consumer durables constitute important items in personal wealth; similarly also, personal cars and all kinds of goods which are connected with their use for holiday purposes.

Concerning these elements of wealth, the already mentioned social research in 1967 discovered that the use of some of them became so widespread that their ownership depended neither on the amount of income nor on membership of a particular social group. This was especially the case with washing machines and television sets. On the other hand, the ownership of a refrigerator turned out to be dependent rather on the level of education, and that of a vacuum cleaner on the quality of flat, which, as has been said earlier, is an independent element of status, often not connected with the amount of income. Ownership of a personal car, however, which still is a comparatively scarce commodity in Czechoslovakia, seems to be, in the first place, a function of income, although this connection is significantly differentiated according to job and education, and to a lesser extent according to the habitat and age of the person concerned.[1]

In general it may be inferred that personal wealth is more differentiated by social groups than is current consumer expenditure. However, this cannot be taken as true with respect to all categories of personal wealth. Basically the per capita

[1] J. Večerník, in *Československá společnost*, pp. 315–16.

living space and the quality of housing conditions including some (not all) consumer durable goods, are more advantageously represented in the social group of employees than in all the other groups. Better housing amenities seem to be the only element of material living standard which can be specified as attributes of a particular socio-economic group.

As stated earlier, all the other differences in material standard are due predominantly to the different per capita income in individual families.

On the other hand, with respect to non-material living standards, the differences in social groups *qua* groups are more conspicuous. Unfortunately statistical records can supply only partial evidence of this phenomenon. They assess on the basis of micro-censuses the participation in cultural performances such as theatres and cinemas and participation in recreational opportunities. Although this participation comprises only a part of the possible range of consumption of cultural values, it is nevertheless significant and in a way representative of the attitude towards culture or a particular type of recreation.

The cultural attendance and recreation pattern in 1965

Table 43

CULTURAL ATTENDANCE AND RECREATION PATTERN
IN 1965
(IN PER CENT OF ALL RESPONDENTS IN THE
RESPECTIVE GROUPS)

	Workers	Employees	Co-operative farmers
Visitors to cinemas	54·2	70·3	41·4
Visitors to theatres	26·9	50·4	27·8
Visitors to concerts	6·6	20·3	4·1
Visitors to sporting events	24·1	32·3	19·3
Holidays in spas or other public recreation centres	3·4	7·2	2·9

Source: CS *Statistical Yearbook* (1968).

(Table 43) reveals that the more sophisticated the type of cultural performance or recreation, the more conspicuous the differences by social groups.

The micro-census results of 1965 were in principle (but not in extent) confirmed by the sample data of 1967 when the utilisation of time spent was investigated. Since in this investigation listening to television or radio is included, the difference in social groups becomes less impressive.

Calculated on a fortnightly basis the time spent on self-education, cultural performances and entertainment (also out-of-doors and at home with television or radio) was in employees' families only 17 per cent higher than in workers' households. In the case of sporting activities, gymnastics, walking and recreation, etc., the difference was even smaller (13 per cent).

However, again as with the income distribution, we may find a significant sex differential in the pattern of cultural consumption. According to the same time utilisation data, women's time spent on the above-mentioned cultural activities or consumption totalled both in workers' and employees' families only 63 per cent of the time spent for the same purposes by men. In sporting activities, gymnastics, walking and recreation, the sex differences were combined with those of social groups. Women workers' participation was 63 per cent of that of men, whereas in employees' households the ratio was much more favourable – 81 per cent.

All this happened in spite of the fact that women spent, as a rule, less time in gainful employment but not as much as expected, i.e. 84·5 per cent of that of men in workers' families and 93·5 per cent in employees' families.

On the other hand, and this is the reason for the lower cultural consumption and recreational activity of women, their engagement in housework (including shopping, small husbandry and maintenance of car) was in both social groups 2·5 times as time consuming as the participation of men in these activities. However, women's care of children required only 21 per cent more time in employees' families and 34 per cent more time in workers' families than the care of children performed by men.[1]

[1] CS *Statistical Yearbook* (1969) p. 456.

If we put together all that we have said up to now on the male/female relationship we realise that women have succeeded in two substantial respects in becoming more equal to men. They now acquire, in greater numbers, a higher education (see Table 32) and are more gainfully employed than ever before. During the twenty years of Communist rule (from 1948 to 1968) women's share in the labour force increased from 37·8 to 46·1 per cent.[1] On the other hand women did not improve their wages in relation to men although they are now, on average, better qualified than previously. Into the bargain they have to carry out a greater part of the work for the household, work which unfortunately is not eased by an adequate supply of service industries.

Concerning the style of life generally, a word should be said on the continuous tendency to strengthen collective forms of living. A new socialist man is supposed to maintain more frequent and livelier contacts with his socialist environment; and in so doing to help, on one side, to further socialist consciousness, and on the other to provide a greater scope for control of anybody's true socialist attitudes. Not only collective extra work (voluntary brigades) but also collective entertainments and recreation are encouraged. To the latter aim trade unions have devoted a good deal of their energy.

Factories, workshops and other premises were found to be the most suitable bases for organisation of collective undertakings. Also within the party and within auxiliary organisations such as Czechoslovak–Soviet Friendship League, the stress shifted more on work in the employment than in the local units. Here the individual was more dependent, more easily supervised and therefore more malleable than at home where he could better take refuge in his family duties.[2] However, even these did not save him from Saturday or Sunday working brigades, activity meant to improve the public surroundings of homes. Although voluntary, the security reasons, with which we shall deal in more detail in the next chapter, made of it often an obligation.

In spite of a considerable wastage of time due to the slow

[1] 25 let, p. 35.
[2] From the middle sixties, however, stress was again also laid on work in local units.

tempo of work and often bad organisation, working brigades did a lot of useful work such as clearing rubbish and building new parks, children's playgrounds, etc., and above all collecting harvest in the country. Individual factories were assigned state or co-operative farms under patronage and provided them with technical help and help in harvest time.

The most intense form of socialist collectivism was found in the so-called Brigades of Socialist Work: workers and employees of a certain working unit obliging themselves not only to work but also to live in a socialist way. The practical meaning of this slogan was summed up by a party official at a conference in 1960, under the following headings: (*a*) striving for higher specialists and general education; (*b*) for better knowledge of Marxism–Leninism; (*c*) for a more active part in collective organisations (trade unions, Association of Youth, Association of Women, Czechoslovak–Soviet Friendship League, etc.); (*d*) collectively attending cultural performances and active participation in cultural creativity; (*e*) taking interest in the family life of members of the collective; (*f*) helping them to overcome the capitalist survivals, to overcome individual vices such as alcoholism, etc., and to acquire new moral attitudes; (*g*) taking care of cultural working environment, for the good quality and nice appearance of products, for the order and cleanliness of working places.[1] After one or two years of successfully practising these socialist manners, the collective is entitled to acquire from a special committee an honorary and noble title, 'Brigade of Socialist Work', and is supposed to provide an example to the rest of the working population.

The campaign to organise Brigades of Socialist Work was launched in 1959 and vigorously sustained in the early sixties. In 1961 there were 71,000 collectives competing for this title, and 8,538 have been awarded it. In 1963 the number of competing collectives increased to almost 89,000 and those who had attained this title exceeded 31,000.[2] The number of members and data on further development have not been disclosed. The whole action, to which great publicity was given, gradually resulted in a kind of formal ritual. Socialist way of life became

[1] *Nová mysl* XIV (1960) p. 180.
[2] CS *Statistical Yearbook* (1964) p. 130.

a matter of written reports rather than of genuine endeavour.

Participation in working brigades at large and the extent of collective forms of life have become the standard tests of socialist behaviour, tests on which often promotion, or even personal rights such as admission of children to higher education or permission to travel abroad (exit visa), were dependent.

The practice of making an individual's enjoyment of constitutional rights dependent on formal tests of conformist behaviour was attenuated in the middle sixties and virtually abolished during the Dubček era. After his fall, however, the former measures have been gradually reimposed, with greater stress being laid on political attitudes; the basic test is the explicit political loyalty to the new régime.

(E) PRESTIGE, SECURITY AND PROSPECTS

Most of the elements of social status dealt with hitherto may be summed up under a common heading – living standard. Only the type and amount of education, the occupation and possibly style of life connected with this lies, in a way, outside the scope of this complex category.

However, all these elements, whether subsumable under the living standard concept or not, may be ingredients of a less tangible but nevertheless significant concept, that of social prestige. In addition the power position – be it in its broad, comprehensive sense, or differentiated into authority and influence – may be a constitutive and often even a determining element of social prestige.

Here a specific problem of value judgement arises. Any position of power derived from a formal post within the establishment can hardly be appreciated without regard to the evaluation of the establishment as a whole. In case of a basic disagreement, especially with a particular activity of the establishment, the social prestige of the position in question might be evaluated by the particular observer in a negative way. This might either develop into a widely accepted custom or it may become a bone of contention, a factor dividing the value attitudes of the society according to the degree of sympathy or antipathy with the particular system. This usually happens in a period of

systemic transformation or wherever force is used in an excessive
way to enforce a particular establishment.

This might be apparently the main reason why, in the
Czechoslovak research on social status, the element of influence
on decision making within the politico-economic sphere did not
reflect a similarly high correlation with a synthetic status index,
as did the other elements of social status such as education level,
complexity of work and style of life.[1]

Resulting from subjective value judgements conceived as an
average or coincidence of the possible majority of them, social
prestige may become an elusive concept for an analyst. On the
other hand it provides the conceptual basis for a complex
synthetic indicator, a basis which unlike any mathematical
formula used for synthesising individual measurements is not
artificial but has a direct sociological meaning.

Nevertheless it is very difficult to imagine the hierarchy of
prestige accepted by the whole population. Different groups
may have other concepts of social importance and usefulness
and even these may fluctuate according to the circumstances.
Any average arrived at is largely dependent on the method of
investigation, especially on the chosen sample, on the questionnaire and on the scoring.

For postwar Czechoslovakia two surveys have been undertaken on this subject (1966 and 1967), the results of which
differ widely, but this is apparently due mainly to the method of
investigation. Whereas the first survey, covering 1,372 respondents (from a sample of 1,400) was centred predominantly on
the social prestige of people with university education,[2] the
other survey of November 1967 (already several times mentioned), based on 13,215 respondents, had a comprehensive
scope and accordingly seems to reflect more plausibly the
standard or average view.

We compare here the results of both surveys (Table 44). In
the first survey the respondents had to rank individual professions according to four subjective criteria: social utility; income
which, in the respondents' view, the representatives of the

[1] Zdeněk Šafář, in *Československá společnost*, p. 67 and passim.
[2] V. Brenner, M. Hrouda, 'Věda a vysokoškolské vzdělání v prestiži
povolání', in *Sociologický časopis* IV (1967) pp. 541–50 and V (1968) pp.
43–54.

professions concerned should get; profession which the respondent considered the most important; and profession which the respondent himself would like to choose without regard to

Table 44

SCALE OF SOCIAL PRESTIGE

Brenner–Hrouda research (1966)		Machonin team research (1967)	
1	Doctor	1	Minister
2	Grammar school teacher	2	Industrial enterprise director
3	Construction engineer	3	Specialist doctor
4	Scientific worker	4	University professor
5	Architect	5	Chairman of a regional government council
6	Co-operative farmer	6	Scientific worker
7	Miner	7	Factory director
8	Nurse	8	Writer
9	Minister	9	Technical supervisor
10	University teacher	10	District attorney
11	Locomotive driver	11	Agronomist
12	Tailor	12	Actor
13	Lathe operator	13	Cabaret artiste
14	Agronomist	14	Grammar school teacher
15	Factory foreman	15	Local doctor (general practitioner)
16	Judge	16	Pharmacist
17	Writer	17	Professional soldier
18	Accountant	18	Chairman of a farmers' co-operative
19	Actor	19	Party official
20	Journalist	20	Construction supervisor
21	Bricklayer	21	Miner
22	Shop assistant	22	T.V. engineer
23	Policeman	23	Restaurant manager
24	Sewage worker	24	Policeman
25	Army officer	25	Factory foreman
26	Labourer	26	Agricultural combine worker
27	Local government official	27	Locomotive driver
28	Typist	28	Elementary school teacher

Table 44 (contd.)

Brenner–Hrouda research (1966)		Machonin team research (1967)	
29	Charwoman	29	Optician
30	Clergyman	30	Foreman bricklayer
		31	Universal lathe operator
		32	Stationmaster
		33	Waiter
		34	Chief of self-service shop
		35	Clergyman
		36	Bricklayer
		37	Locksmith
		38	Tool grinder
		39	Decorator
		40	Nurse
		41	Public librarian
		42	Asphalt layer
		43	Hairdresser
		44	Train conductor
		45	Petrol pump attendant
		46	Postman
		47	Member of co-operative farm working group
		48	Railway signal box man
		49	Labourer
		50	Car park attendant

material benefit. Sums of points scored in these four evaluations represented the final result of the hierarchy of prestige.

In the second case the procedure was the other way round; the assignment of individual professions within the hierarchy scale of social prestige was left over to the individual respondents whose comments on this issue (received by about half of them, though mainly from respondents of lower education) served to ascertain the main criteria involved in their valuation; they were mainly ordered according to their income, type of work, social utility, qualification, personal experience, quality of performance and responsibility – but also in some cases from primitive animosity (this in 3 per cent of responses).[1]

It is significant that the respondents did not dwell too much on the appreciation of power position as an element of social prestige. This corroborates our hypothesis on the disputed view as to whether the power position in itself is of positive value. On the other hand the same respondents agreed to ascribe certain power positions to the highest ranks in the whole scheme. However, these were representing the traditional functions such as ministers, enterprise managers, and so on, and not functions connected with the apparat of the Communist Party, which both formally and factually is the leading power in the society. (The party official ranks in nineteenth place among fifty.)

The subjective value of a certain social status or its specific elements may diminish with the insecurity of the position attained. Security in this respect is usually understood as security in holding a particular job and, in case of incapacity because of illness, accident, old age or unemployment, receiving an adequate compensatory income. This kind of security is usually provided by two means of legal safeguards. First, by the laws regulating the conditions of hiring and firing in employment, and second by the range of people and cases covered by the social insurance schemes.

However, in political régimes where ideological homogeneity becomes one of the main principles of policy, there is a danger of being not only fired for the usual reasons ensuing from socio-economic relationships in employment but, and this especially in cases of non-manual and better paid jobs, for political reasons as well. This widens the range of insecurity in a direction which as a matter of principle cannot be covered by any insurance measure other than the required compliance of employees in political matters, genuine or feigned. We have to bear in mind this double meaning of social security if we want to do justice to a particular society.

In postwar Czechoslovakia the development of social security became in this respect highly dichotomic. On one side the social insurance scheme providing sickness, invalid and similar benefits and old-age pensions, already extended during the

[1] Jaroslav Kapr, 'Obecná struktura prestiže povolání v Československu', in *Československá společnost*, pp. 394–5.

prewar republic, was further expanded. It gradually covered all population working in employment, in co-operatives, and as self-employed artists or scientific workers.[1] The other self-employed population is covered only partly (in 1968 35,000 persons out of 164,000) and by the old-age scheme only. The comprehensive national insurance scheme also includes maternity aids and family allowances.

To see the intensity of these measures, the extent of the most frequent benefits have to be reviewed; sickness benefits depend on the length of employment and vary in the first three days of sickness between 50 and 70 per cent and later between 60 and 90 per cent of the previous wage net of taxes. Pensions are scaled according to the type of work and length of employment between 50 and 70 per cent of previous average earnings.[2] Family allowances are progressively scaled according to the number of children, giving 90 Kčs (equivalent of slightly over £2) per month for one child, 330 Kčs for two children, 680 Kčs for three and 1030 Kčs (circa £26) for four children; for each addition child the allowance is increased by 240 Kčs (about £6 per month).[3]

Although, with the exception of unemployment (which is supposed not to be possible in a socialist society), the coverage of potential risks is comprehensive, the magnitude of these benefits is not always a social safeguard to the people concerned. We have already mentioned the position of pensioners who often wanting to preserve their income above the poverty level have to take on part-time jobs. Still less adequate are the family allowances, especially expenditure for the first child, which is usually the highest in the family. It is a well-known fact that the living standard of families getting a first or second child usually suffer a considerable setback.

Nevertheless despite these shortcomings this type of social security has a nation-wide coverage and in principle is not differentiated according to the social groups. Only some cate-

[1] As shown earlier, this group of self-employed intellectuals is a tiny one (3,300 persons in 1969) and is not independent in the usual sense, but depends on regulations transmitted to them from Party organs by their specific official professional organisations.

[2] Introductory note to the corresponding section in CS *Statistical Yearbooks*.

[3] Igor Tomeš *et al.*, *Československé právo sociálneho zabezpečenia* (Bratislava, 1969) p. 248.

gories enjoy preferential treatment with regard to age and/or amount of pensions (e.g. miners, people who work with dangerous materials, policemen, etc.), while – until the early sixties – people sentenced for serious offences (often for political reasons) would have lost their accumulated claims on the old age funds. In general it may be inferred that national insurance provides another channel for the levelling of social status. Only the so-called personal pensions granted to people with outstanding merits make an exception from this rule.

On the other hand the engagement and dismissal conditions are not levelled so far. Although the labour code does not differentiate between social groups it is not the only source of rules regulating employment conditions. As stated earlier there is another line of supervision provided by special officials who have to decide whether or not people with nonconformist political or religious attitudes may be acceptable for particular jobs. This type of screening is understandably most important with respect to responsible jobs, with positions of decision making, be it in industry or in other branches of social life. Of all the social groups which we can identify in this study it is in the first place employees, and among them intelligentsia, who are most subjected to political scrutiny. The main reason being political and ideological conformity, it is obvious that cultural intelligentsia becomes the main target of periodical purges.

Thus in comparison with the prewar period the social security pattern was turned upside down. Before the war the lower the qualification the greater the insecurity of employment. After 1948 the greater security of employment in lower-qualified jobs was matched by a greater insecurity of qualified people unless they belonged to a comparatively small group of highly qualified technicians in short supply and necessary for strategic reasons. However, even these might have found 'social security' in Solzhenitsyn's *First Circle*.

A sense of security may be envisaged as a complementary element of living standard not only with respect to individuals but to the whole of the family. Social security schemes cover, as a rule, wives and children up to a certain age dependent on the period of training; similarly acts of political conformity are taken on behalf of, or with regard to, family prospects. As will be shown in the next chapter, there was a much greater proportion of Communist Party members among the fathers of families than in the rest of the population. In 1967 the difference was of staggering magnitude – 33·0 to 4·2 per cent.[1] This may only be partly due to greater genuine interest in politics by people in responsible family positions. Partly, and probably to a greater extent, the means of another kind of social insurance might be seen in this difference.

The important element of this type of insurance is the responsibility for education of children. As we have already demonstrated in Chapter 2 (B), the prospects of obtaining a higher education, especially at university level, depended much on class origin or on political attitude, not only of the people concerned, but very often of their parents. The emphasis on this aspect somewhat relaxed during the middle sixties but since 1970 it has been reimposed. On the other hand the purges and voluntary resignations from the party, which have deprived it of almost a third of its membership, are reducing the number of persons insured in this way for these particular contingencies.

Party membership is of course not only a means of security but also a precondition for promotion in particular jobs. The importance of party membership in acquiring a certain position within the power structure will be discussed in the next chapter. Here we would like only to state that historically this condition preceded the other one which, from about the middle sixties, became important as well, namely, that of education.

As we have already shown in chapter 2 (B) and will show in more detail in the next chapter, there were a number of people in higher positions without adequate education, who totalled in 1962 almost the half-million mark (about 9 per cent of the labour force). They were induced to complete their education. There were a considerable number of participants in evening and part-time courses. From 1962 to 1968 31,000 of them obtained degrees and 173,000 completed their vocational studies on secondary level.[2] However in 1970 there were still 182,470 persons without higher, and 299,903 without secondary education in posts with these educational requirements.[3]

[1] For details see p. 117.

[2] There were also cases where the attaining of a degree was a matter of political pressure rather than a result of genuine studies.

[3] CS *Statistical Yearbook* (1971) p. 142.

There is of course a natural tendency to encourage children to a higher position of social status and social prestige than that of the parents. The usual means to attain it is the enrolment for a higher level of education. However, according to the data at our disposal, it does not seem that there is only a one-way traffic in this respect. According to the sociological research in 1967 there were also quite frequent cases of intergenerational downward mobility. Only about a half of sons of fathers with university education reached the educational level of their fathers. Sons of fathers with completed secondary education followed their fathers in about 42 per cent of respondents whereas the rest was about equally divided between promotion and demotion, which in most cases was by more than one degree. Sons of fathers with lower vocational education did not even attain this level of education in about a third of cases. In general the authors of the research state that the frequency of attaining a lower level of education than the father's was greater in the present than in the previous generation.[1]

This downward movement was, however, still outweighed by the upward movement from the strata with a lower educational level, an upward movement which until then was the main reason for the growing proportion of population with higher education. Nevertheless the magnitude of the countervailing downward mobility is striking. It is hard to say how far it was due to a realistic appreciation of the difference between fathers' and sons' capacity to study and how far it was, in 1967, still due to the political barrier to higher education; or how far it was that the levelling of incomes now offered equally good prospects to skilled workers as to those with higher education; or how far, possibly, the prospect of a greater social security on a lower educational level played a subsidiary role.

(f) POSITION WITHIN THE POWER STRUCTURE

In deciding to leave this particular element of social status to the end of our review of the new stratification pattern, we did so not because of its minor importance. On the contrary, we found

---

[1] Josef Alan, 'Úloha vzdělání v sociální diferenciaci naší společnosti', in *Československá Společnost*, pp. 287–8.

it most decisive and significant for the social system, or to use a more explicit term, for the politico-economic formation which eventually asserted itself in postwar Czechoslovakia.

In order to do full justice to the relevance of this aspect we have found it expedient to deal first with all other attributes of social status, in which, as demonstrated, a tendency towards levelling and towards homogenisation prevailed as a rule. With the exception of sex and productive and non-productive age differences there was, in the long run, a considerable narrowing of differentials. Where the complexity of work and responsibility of job did not admit of hiring less qualified or even non-qualified personnel, such as in technology or in medicine, there was at least a clear-cut tendency to diminish all other differentials connected with these particular professions. The partial reversal of this tendency with the turn of the decade (1950/60) did not develop far enough to change appreciably the egalitarian pattern. Nevertheless some categories of intelligentsia (especially the educationalists) got a considerably better treatment.

On the other hand, the structure of power positions was not redistributed towards greater equality, but on the contrary within a few years after 1948 acquired a distinct and steep differentiation with all the important decision making concentrated in a comparatively small body at the top. To review this development in possibly the most tangible terms, we have to turn first to the changed form of ownership.

As is well known the form of ownership does not reveal the whole truth about the position of those who have to operate the means of production. However meaningful the socialisation might have been to the expropriated owners, it might not bring corresponding change to the workers. The concept of the whole nation as the owner means little in tangible terms. What is important is who is actually controlling the objects of ownership; in the case of means of production, who controls access to them (who decides about employment of persons), who provides management, who disposes of the output and who decides on the distribution of proceeds. *Pace* Dahrendorf's poignant criticism of Burnham's theory as a whole,[1] there is a good deal of truth in the latter's thesis that the main sociologi-

[1] Ralf Dahrendorf, *Class and Class Conflict in Industrial Society* (London, 1969) pp. 87–92.

cally relevant point of ownership is the actual control.[1] Even if it does not involve the dispositional right to sell the property and if the holding of the position of control depends on another person's decision, for all other persons working with the objects of that ownership, the attributes of control are most important.

The promoters of the social change in 1945 in Czechoslovakia seem to have been aware of this fact. Shades of opinion concerning the factual exercise of ownership rights were dispersed along the line, on the one end of which was the Workers' Council elected by the direct suffrage of all employees, and on the other the management by technico-economic experts. In the general mood of enthusiasm and speed with which all measures had to be taken, the difference could not polarise to the extent which it did in 1968 when the Workers' Councils campaign clashed with the vested interests of the established management. In 1945 neither technocrats nor co-operative socialists – the first scattered across all the political parties of those days, the second represented mainly by the trade union representatives – did not push their demands to the extreme. The outcome was a compromise solution; a decree following in the wake of the first phase of nationalisation (October 1945) established in every factory, institute or office with more than fifty employees the factory or employee council composed of the elected representatives of workers and employees with the task of 'guaranteeing the smooth operation of the enterprise' (a revolutionary decree thus put beyond any doubt that it intended to create a non-revolutionary institution). The factory council had to ensure that the enterprise was operating in accordance with the public interest (salut public!) and with the social and cultural interests of the employees. The councils were, in particular, entitled to take part in the decision making on wages and salaries and to co-operate in the hiring and firing of employees, in short, in matters which are now labelled as human relations in the West. Management was obliged to contribute 10 per cent of net profits to the council's special fund.

The factory and employees' councils were put under the guidance of trade unions which on one side provided them with efficient support and technical advice, but on the other was a limiting factor in their self-determination. The Trade Union

[1] James Burnham, *The Managerial Revolution* (London, 1945) p. 81.

Council of those days represented a big political and economic power largely profiting from the Nazi heritage, i.e. an enforced unification of the prewar, widely split trade unions.

As after February 1948 the trade unions became – to use Stalin's own appropriate term – the 'transmission belt' of the Communist leadership and government, their function consisted then rather in implementing party and government decisions. Factory and employees' councils lost not only their independence but also any significance as defenders of genuine workers' interests in relation to the management.

Similarly the workers' militia, organised as the working class army in 1945, became more of a Party army. It is significant that a draft of a bill on the workers' militia, submitted to the Presidium of the Central Committee of the Communist Party on 27 September 1948, was not, for undisclosed reasons, approved. Instead it was the Ministry of the Interior which was by the law of 21 December 1948 entrusted with the organisation of the workers' militia.[1]

The change could not be better illustrated than by the main highlights of workers' intercessions within the five-year period 1948–53. In February 1948 the majority of the trade unionists' delegates supported a further wave of nationalisation (only a minority of opponents during the famous Factory Council Congress voted against).[2] At the end of 1951, when the annual bonuses (thirteenth salary paid before Christmas) were abolished, the workers in some factories (e.g. Brno) decided to strike and were completely abandoned by their official class organs – trade unions and workers' militia. The same happened during the subsequent abolition of the traditional income in kind which had provided workers, especially in food manufacturing, with considerable additional income. This development reached its climax during the 1953 monetary reform when the

---

[1] Ivan Škurlo, *Február a ľudové milície* (Bratislava, 1968) pp. 118–19.

[2] It is difficult to assess what was the genuine proportion of no-votes on this occasion. As the participants in this event testify, the atmosphere was very militant, the delegates came in already under this influence and A. Zápotocký being in the chair, counted the votes (they were delivered by acclamation) arbitrarily, admitting only a fragment of the hands lifted for the no-vote with apparent contempt for the powerless opposition. This behaviour was the more ominous as there was no doubt that the number of votes in favour of the resolution were in a clear majority.

Prague workers' militia was sent to Plzeň to help to suppress the workers' riots there.

However, neither did the technocrats win their way. The technical and scientific experts had to play second fiddle. Supreme control was taken by Party officials. The latter were vested not only with the power of final decision on the draft of economic plans but also with economic policy and the employment of the experts themselves who thus became completely dependent on the political apparat. Gradually a situation developed leading eventually, in 1968, to an unexpected and paradoxical alliance between some technocratically minded elements and the promoters of workers councils. Both had a common master hampering equally – although in different ways – their aspirations for greater scope for action and self-determination.

It is worth while to inquire into this development in more detail, and as far as possible to express it, in quantitative terms. On one side, as mentioned earlier, we can follow a rapid growth of labour qualifications both at higher and secondary education levels. The number of specialists per thousand of labour force in the socialist sector of economy (farmers' co-operatives not included) increased from 104 in 1953 to 197 in 1966,[1] i.e. within thirteen years almost doubled. How far the greater number of people with higher or secondary education asserted themselves in leading positions will be shown later (see pp. 113–14).

Before that we have to estimate the number of persons who were, after the socialisation had been completed, in effective control of the means of production. Their number can be assessed for several years during the sixties, for which data covering about 60 per cent of economy (in terms of persons engaged) were published in sufficient detail. The respective figures for the rest of the economy can be obtained from the number of units (shops, workshops and other premises in operation). The result with the respective breakdowns is given in Table 45.

Although these people are in the most direct control of the means of production, they are not in full command of them. Being in charge of enterprises which have to be operated according to the plan, their control of them is limited to the

[1] 25 let, p. 40.

Table 45

PERSONS IN DIRECT CONTROL OF THE MEANS OF PRODUCTION IN 1966/7

1	Directors and deputy directors in industry, construction and the state sector of agriculture	14,085*
2	Directors and deputy directors in other branches of the state sector	1,710†
3	Chairmen of farmers' co-operatives	6,463‡
4	Divisional managers in industry, construction and the state sector of agriculture	36,262*
5	Divisional managers in other branches of the state sector	4,402[1]
6	Other managerial and supervisory personnel in production	28,997*
7	Chiefs of retail shop units	67,267‡
8	Chiefs of restaurants and other catering services	33,203‡
9	Chiefs of hotels and other accommodation units	3,028‡
10	Chiefs of communal service units	3,681‡
11	Chiefs of building and housing co-operatives	717‡
12	Total	199,815
13	In per cent of the number of households (4,390 thousand in 1967)	4·6 per cent

* Number of persons as reported by CS *Statistical Yearbooks* for 1966.
† Number of persons as reported by *Economico-Political Manual* for 1967 (*Hospodářski-politická rukověť*, Prague, 1967).
‡ Number of units as reported by CS *Statistical Yearbooks* for 1966.
[1] Estimate based on the assumption that the number of divisional managers is in the same ratio to directors and deputy directors as in 1 and 4.

implementation of orders from above. We have, therefore, to add to our table that part of the government and party apparat which is concerned with the plan and economic decisions. With a complete lack of any data, we have to do it in the light of personal experience, and put the final figure tentatively between 3,000 and 5,000 persons. This may bring the total to 205,000.

Even so we get a figure which is much less than the half a million persons who owned enterprises employing hired labour or farms above 10 ha. before the war.[1] This indicates a steeper distribution of economic power than was the case before the war. No wonder, since so many technical and managerial units were amalgamated. Before the war there were, at the end of 1937, 1,995 joint stock and share holder companies operating in mining and manufacturing and more than 70,000 enterprises with workers covered by accident insurance. In 1969 there were in mining and manufacturing 871 large national enterprises and 690 co-operative and local industry units.[2] Thus the number of big industrial enterprises was reduced to less than half and the number of small enterprises to 1 per cent. In agriculture over 200,000 farms with more than 10 ha. land were fused into less than 7,000 co-operatives.

However, the amalgamation of enterprises and concentration of capital was only one cause of the concentration of managerial power. The substitution of the planned for the market economy operated in the same direction. As a result of the centrally planned economy, the decision making on the enterprise level was reduced to finding out the best ways of fulfilling the targets fixed by a higher authority. Decisions on the volume and variety of output, on prices, wages and investment were concentrated at the government level; although often divided among individual ministries or ministerial commissions, they were always closely supervised by the corresponding section of the central party apparat.

Thus the scope of power ensuing from the control of the means of production, became, in comparison with private ownership, much more hierarchised. Although often commanding larger

[1] Data from 1930 adjusted by the results of the 1946 census with respect to enterprises employing 3–5 persons. Source: CS *Statistical Yearbooks* (1934–8) and *Sociální struktura socialistické společnosti*, p. 515.
[2] CS *Statistical Yearbooks* (1941) pp. 175 and 182; (1970) pp. 220 and 374.

units, managers are less in command of them than the former capitalists. On the other hand, at the top level, the scope of managerial power extends much further than that of any capitalist.

It should not be forgotten however that the position of, socialist managers, even of the most powerful ones at the top, is in principle less stable. It is dependent neither on their property rights nor, as a rule, on their economic fortunes but on their political reliability, on their merits for the system and possibly on their achievements in the position concerned, achievements the main criteria of which are fulfilment of the indicators of the economic plans, which only occasionally may coincide with usual business-type considerations.

However, these are technical or professional rather than social aspects of the work and position of socialist managers. On the other hand their social position – that is, position in terms of attributes of status, such as prestige, influence, living standard and style of life – does not differ appreciably from that of former capitalists. So far they have not developed a new 'socialist' way of life; they have rather been eager to emulate the bourgeois standard. From this point of view they constitute a stratum which might well be described as a 'salaried bourgeoisie'.

Now, according to what criteria does the individual become entrusted with the control of the means of production? Wesolowski, trying to find the main differences in the social stratification of countries with different socio-economic systems, puts forward the following hypothesis:

In socialist society the position of each and everyone is largely determined by his occupational status and the latter depends greatly on his education and on skills following from this education. And because there is a direct bond between occupation on the one hand and income and social prestige on the other, education represents an important instrument for obtaining other values.[1]

However, this hypothesis sounds – in the light of Czechoslovakia's experience – like a normative rather than a factual statement. It is a well known fact that the main precondition of access to power in such a socialist state as Wesolowski has in mind is party membership, and within this preference has been

---

[1] W. Wesolowski, 'The Notions of Strata and Class in Socialist Society', published in *Social Inequality* (London, 1969) pp. 141–42.

given to people of working-class origin. In Czechoslovakia class origin and political reliability were until 1967, and largely again since 1969, the main conditions required not only for the most responsible jobs, but for promotion in a wide range of jobs in all branches of economic and cultural activity. Even when a higher qualification was required those with better political and class qualification had the advantage over equally or even better qualified competitors in their speciality.

This kind of discrimination has been claimed to be a necessary prerequisite of defending the system against its class enemies. It was supposed that with time the working class would supply qualified personnel of its own, who, being politically reliable, would gradually take over all jobs requiring higher qualification. How far the supposition that working-class origin is the best guarantee of political loyalty works in practice, will be touched in the concluding chapter. Here we shall enquire how far education became the main precondition of attaining control of the means of production, in a period when Czechoslovak society has been already proclaimed as being socialist, i.e. in the sixties.

Statistical data are available for the technico-economic cadres in industry, construction, forestry and the state sector in agriculture (first group in Table 45), i.e. in enterprises representing about 60 per cent of the labour force in the economic sphere. These comprehensive figures available for 1962, 1963 and 1966 can be supplemented by and checked against results of a widely conceived and thoroughgoing sociological investigation undertaken in November 1967, dealing with a sample of 13·215 persons.[1] Both sources provide us with consistent information.

According to the comprehensive data, of the directors and deputy directors only 42·8 per cent in 1962 and 44·8 per cent in 1966 had the required qualification for these responsible jobs; in the category of leaders of management divisions the percentage was 45·5 in 1962 and 48·3 in 1966. Among the leaders of

[1] Number of respondents chosen from the standard panel sample of one per cent of heads of households (used by the State Statistical Office) by means of random two-stage selection. For further details see Zdeněk Šafář, 'Základní metodologická východiska šetření', in *Československá společnost* (Bratislava, 1969) pp. 49 and ff.

production departments there were at the beginning still less qualified 'cadres' – 37·8 per cent in 1962; but in 1966 they acquired approximately the same proportion in the whole as the above-mentioned groups – 47·2 per cent. Also low was the percentage of qualification for foremen, but here there was still more clear-cut improvement within the four years, from 35·6 per cent in 1962 to 48·7 in 1966. Apparently, and significantly, on the lower level the intended change was more feasible. On the other hand qualified labour at the enterprise and factory level was better represented in the rank and file technical personnel: 55·7 per cent in 1962 and 58·6 per cent in 1966; not however in the administrative personnel: 37·2 in 1962 and 42·6 per cent in 1966.

According to the sample (Autumn 1967), of the chiefs and their deputies in all organisations (i.e. not only those covered by the comprehensive data) only 48·4 per cent had a higher or completed secondary education.[1]

The inadequate qualification of economic managers was one of many side issues of the economic reform in the middle sixties and also one of the main obstacles to its implementation.

Unfortunately, there are no data on the qualification of the technico-economic personnel at the ministerial or party level. However, some conjectures may be made from the sociological survey already mentioned, which includes also representatives of these groups.

Furthermore, we can get from this survey a general view of the importance of Communist Party membership for the aquisition of leading positions. There is no wonder that it is so, because the Communist Party is the cornerstone of the whole system. It is explicitly embodied in the constitution, the fourth article of which reads: 'The guiding force in society and in the State is the vanguard of the working class, the Communist Party of Czechoslovakia, a voluntary militant alliance of the most active and most politically conscious citizens from the ranks of the workers, farmers and intelligentsia.'[2] Thus it might be expected a priori that the higher the position the more likely party members are to be vested with it. This supposition is

[1] Josef Alan, 'Úloha vzdělání v sociální diferenciaci naší společnosti', in *Československá společnost*, p. 278.
[2] Quoted from the official English translation (Prague, 1964).

fully corroborated by empirical data collected by the survey quoted above. In juxtaposition with other indicators they offer a more penetrating and accurate insight into the power structure of a Soviet-type socialist society.

The researchers chose to see the problem of power as embodied in two aspects: that of *authority*, i.e. power resulting from professional positions in the establishment, and that of *influence*, i.e. power resulting from elected functions and/or from membership in influential organisations.[1] Although election in a Soviet-type socialist society is not equivalent to election in the West it does, nevertheless represent (even if openly manipulated) a line of possible promotion, alternative to promotion on a professional scale. Functions acquired by such an 'election' can be either purely formal or really influential according to the circumstances, i.e. mainly according to the personal status of the person concerned within the party hierarchy.

Data collected in the research indicate (*a*) the pyramid of power, in both its components, (*b*) the share of Communists in its individual brackets (Table 46).

Table 46

LEVEL OF POWER AND MEMBERSHIP OF THE
COMMUNIST PARTY IN 1967

Level of power	Percentage of respondents		Percentage of Communists	
	Authority	Influence	Authority	Influence
1	2	—	72 ⎫	40
2	3	1	65 ⎰	
3	16	3	47	70
4	27	26	34	60
5	52	70	24	20
Total	100	100	33	33

Source: Graphs in L. Brokl, in *Československá společnost*, pp. 243 and 258. As in the source, numeric values are not given: figures had to be derived from graphs and therefore accepted with approximate accuracy. However, the order of differences is wide enough to enable reliable conclusions.

[1] For the further elucidation of concepts, see Lubomír Brokl, 'Moc a sociální rozvrstvení', in *Československá společnost*, p. 239.

The pyramid of power is steeper with respect to influence ('elected' functions) than with respect to authority (professional positions). On the other hand, in view of what is known from other sources, the real power is predominantly situated in the professional positions, or in positions where profession (e.g. in party apparat) is closely connected with function (such as in government).

Within the sample, Party members are also more represented in the upper brackets of authority than of influence. Here the largest share of Communists is on a lower level of power, where the 'elected' functionaries have apparently the widest range of actual power, as is the case with local government and local trade unions. Elected functions as shown in the higher brackets of Table 46 are represented to such a small extent that the data on party membership are not conclusive. We have to check them against other sources of information.

It is not difficult to do so and to complete Table 46 with relevant indicators on the composition of the three constitutionally highest bodies in the state, nominally all of them elected, i.e. Parliament, Government and the Presidium of the Central Committee of the Communist Party, which virtually wields the supreme power in the state. In Parliament 74 per cent were Communists, in the Government at ministerial level 92 per cent, and in the Central Committee, of course, 100 per cent.

However, in evaluating the above-mentioned stratification of power in connection with membership of the Communist Party, we have to bear in mind that the whole sample shows a much higher percentage of Communists than their share in the total population above 18, which is the age from which party membership is possible. Whereas in the sample referred to one-third were Communists, in the whole adult population only 16·9 were Communist Party members.[1]

This difference is obviously due to the fact that the sample includes only the head of households, i.e. married men with families ('socialised men' as the authors of the research label them) and within this group the older generation and 'fuller'

[1] According to official information there were 1,690,799 members of the Communist Party at 1 January 1968 in Czechoslovakia. As the data of the survey relates to November 1967, the figures are fairly comparable.

stable households are slightly over-represented.[1] A higher proportion of party members among these people is most plausible and, in a way, as hinted at already in the previous chapter, can be seen as an indicator of 'existential' considerations, an indicator of Party membership as a safeguard of better promotion for the head of the family and the children alike.

When we now deduct from the number of all members of the Communist Party (1,691 thousand) those who are covered by the sample of heads of households (33 per cent of 4,390 thousand) we get only 242 thousand Communists left, which represents only 4·2 per cent of the remaining (i.e. more or less dependent) population.[2] The pyramid, with the growing proportion of Communists from 4·2 per cent at the bottom to 100 per cent at the top, is thus complete.[3]

Another important feature which can be seen from the comparison of the comprehensive data with the results of the survey is the relative strength of economic and non-economic managers. As the sample covers people working in all spheres of occupation, its highest category includes not only persons who are in control of the means of production but also people who are in control of the means of education, cultural diffusion, health, defence and repression.

These groups conceived as authority holders on the level of

---

[1] Z. Šafář, in *Československá společnost*, p. 50.

[2] This supposition is confirmed by partial data, such as data on the proportion of Party members among the recruits, data quoted at the eleventh Congress of the Communist Party in June 1958. According to the minutes of this Congress it was complained that there were only 5·2 per cent of Communists in the conscription year 1953 and still less, 3·3 per cent, in the conscription year 1957. Despite all the propaganda the yearly acquisition of new members into the Party made only 3·5 per cent of the levies (*Protokol XI. řádného sjezdu* KSČ, (Prague, 1958) p. 216).

[3] The extrapolation of the pyramid of power in both directions, from the bottom to the top level, corroborates the basic tendency of the results of the survey, which – as its authors explicitly state – did not include these upper, in a way key, positions (L. Brokl, in *Československá společnost*, p. 241) and in dealing only with the heads of households did not include the lowest strata from the point of view of power. With respect to this, Petrusek's comment on this particular issue (*Sociologický časopis*, V (1969) p. 586), claiming a less pronounced dependence of access to authority on party membership than expected, seems not to be justified.

organisations' bosses comprise 15·4 per cent of the sample,[1] whereas persons in control of the means of production calculated on the basis of comprehensive data (see Table 46) constitute – with the inclusion of managers on the ministerial, local government and party level – only about 5 per cent of the corresponding total of heads of households. The difference may be partly due to a more restricted definition of economic managers in our table but partly also to the greater weight of leading positions outside the economic sphere.

The authors of the research confirm this second hypothesis. They state that the majority of the positions of power within the sample are concentrated in the fields of culture, health, public administration and the army.[2] If this reflects the true relationships in the society (and in view of what has been already said, there is little doubt about it), it reveals an important factor in the socialist establishment in Czechoslovakia, i.e. the greater representation of positions of power within the superstructure – to use Marx's terminology – than within the economic basis. The relative importance of superstructure is further underlined by a higher participation of party members in its positions of power.[3]

As another indicator of the hierarchy of roles in postwar Czechoslovakia the social composition of the parliament, which is supposed to be a representative body of the socialist society, may be shown. The fact that its members are selected at different party levels and finally approved by the National Front, which is the platform where the Communist Party representatives inform their colleagues of the rump-parties about the roles assigned to them, does not invalidate this supposition; as the voters are not in a position to bring about any alterations, the geometry of representation can be designed the more rationally according to the principle desired. Thus the social composition of the parliament may serve, in a way, as an indicator of the political relevance ascribed to the various groups.

Of the 300 members in 1967, 18·7 per cent were workers, 18·7 per cent were members or chairmen of farmers' co-operatives, 9·7 per cent belonged to the technical intelligentsia, 12·3 per cent to the cultural intelligentsia, 3·3 per cent were

---

[1] L. Brokl, in *Československá společnost*, p. 255.
[2] Ibid. p. 257.   [3] Ibid.

retired and 0·3 per cent were housewives; on the other hand 37 per cent were members of the apparat, of which 33·7 per cent were in the apparat of the party and government and 3·3 per cent in the army and security forces.[1]

It has been already shown in the previous chapters what kind of changes in occupation pattern took place in postwar Czechoslovakia (Table 17). Some of them followed the general trends in industrially developed societies such as the decline of persons engaged in agriculture, and the increase in education, health, science and research and general administrative personnel. Some of them are peculiar to the Soviet type of socialist societies, some to totalitarian states generally: slow development of economic services characterises the first type only, and the development of a strong repressive apparat both of them equally. (However, our figures do not reflect all changes in this respect, they leave aside the para-military organisation of workers' militia, which adds substantially to the strength of internal security forces.)

In following the changes in the employment pattern we have further to bear in mind that the technical means at the disposal of individual occupations also increased considerably, though in very different proportions.

The greatest beneficiaries of fast-developing technology are industry and the armed forces. Therefore, the productive force of industry and the striking power of the army and security forces has increased far more than indicate the increase of people engaged. To a certain extent also, education has benefited from the introduction of new techniques such as new mass media which, in terms of coverage of human free time, attained almost the upper limit of possibilities.

However, the most important aspect is the relevance of roles which the various professions or occupations have attained within the society.

In a Soviet type of socialist society, decisions on all essentials of societal life are made by the supreme body of the Communist Party. At the top level there is no autonomous economic and cultural policy, both of them are subordinated to political considerations. These for their part might have considerable economic and cultural implications, they may even be expressed

[1] *Hospodářsko-politická rukověť'*, I, p. 103.

in economic or cultural terms as is the vision of a communist society in the future; however, they are as a matter of principle, derived from Marxist–Leninist doctrine – and all the concentrated power of the Communist Party and of the state it dominates has to be used for their implementation.

As the basic societal aims are supposed to be, once for all, scientifically substantiated, and as the supreme body of the Party is supposed to be the only rightful interpreter of the doctrine, they are never put to a genuine public test. On the contrary, the public's conformity with the declared aims of the leadership and its readiness to perform extra brigade work for these aims is considered to be the basic test of its loyalty to the state and socialist society.

Thus the means of ideological education and the means of compulsion acquire a much greater weight in the government services and a higher priority in the society in general than in any society where the spontaneous interests and endeavours of individuals are more trusted and where the functioning of their uncontrolled groups is not only permitted but also safeguarded by an appropriate system of mutual power balances.

Under these conditions it is understandable that the majority of the positions of power in postwar Czechoslovakia have been concentrated not in the economy but, as the previously mentioned survey and other data have shown, in the 'superstructure', and within it in the prominent Party members operating in close contact with the Party apparat.

Theoretically of course it is maintained that the Communist Party is the vanguard of the working class and that it is through this vanguard that the working class is actually ruling the state and society, exercising thus the dictatorship of the proletariat, which is the true essence of people's democracy. In fact, the Communist Party was composed predominantly of workers only before it assumed the absolute power within the state. Whereas in 1946 the proportion of active workers in its membership was 57 per cent,[1] in 1956 it dropped to 36[2] and in 1966 to only 33 per cent.[3]

[1] E. Dvořáková, P. Lesjuk, *ČS společnost a komunisté v letech 1945–1948* (Prague, 1967) p. 71.

[2] A. Novotný, *Projevy a stati 1, 1954–1957* (Praha, 1964) p. 349.

[3] *XIII. Sjezd Komunistické strany Československa* (Praha, 1967) p. 911.

Nevertheless, there were several channels through which workers could acquire decisive positions within the state – and, as a rule, ceased to be workers. First, there was the party apparat itself, where most of the older generation were workers. Second, there were officials entrusted with supervision of the employment policy in organisations and enterprises (we shall return to them shortly) who were mostly of working-class origin. Similarly, the people's judges and a great many of the security police were recruited from the working class. Also, many responsible jobs in factory management were reserved for workers. Although they were encouraged to improve their qualifications by means of evening courses, which many of them did, there remained nevertheless, as was shown on page 104, many more who refrained from doing so. In addition, as mentioned earlier, there was a continuing tendency to give preference to workers' children in admission to secondary and higher education. Discrimination against applicants of bourgeois origin affected of course only the prewar ruling classes or non-conformist elements and not, as can be seen from Table 18, the new 'salaried bourgeoisie' or managerial class who emerged at the top of the new establishment.

All these measures brought – as already demonstrated (see p. 45) – a great number of former workers,[1] and later on sons and daughters of workers, to responsible positions. However, there was not only a tendency to facilitate the access of members of the working class to responsible jobs in the economy and the apparat, but to promote all the workers' occupations, especially those in heavy industry and without an adequate supply of labour, to a higher level of prestige. Workers in extraction and heavy industries have been especially extolled. A slogan 'I am a miner, who is more?' was coined and several psychological devices were invented to bolster the prestige and self-confidence of miners and metal workers. Although this policy brought some material advantages to these particular and uncontestably difficult occupations (see Table 27) not much could be achieved

[1] These people did not come as a rule from the hard-core of the working class, such as skilled workers in general or workers in heavy industry in particular, but were often recruited from less typical or less personally successful workers' ranks. Political activity, which implied an uncritical and unwavering adherence to the Party line, was the main prerequisite.

to bolster their prestige, as it was precisely these two kinds of labour to which the largest number of convicts (for political, economic and other reasons) were assigned. In many mines and metal mills, free workers, nominally constituting the workers' aristocracy, worked side by side with convict labour. This fact could not but cast serious doubt on the whole pyramid of prestige within which the miners should be at the top. As shown in the previous chapter (Table 44), miners ranked in the hierarchy of social prestige at the seventh place among thirty according to one study and at twenty-first place among fifty according to another. However, this is only one example of the gulf between the wishes and realities.

On a more general plane there was – again contrary to official wishes – a growing feeling that those who were former workers and had acquired high jobs within the apparat, had gradually lost their class character as workers and acquired features of the new class or at least of the new leading group, the power of whom consisted in the control either of the means of production or, to use Ossowski's apposite term, of the 'means of compulsion'.[1]

This estrangement was gradual and was felt – quite in agreement with R. Dahrendorf's theorem[2] – rather by those below, the ruled, than those above, the ruling ones. Although the belief of the former workers, now apparatchiks of the party, that they were still good sons of the working class might have been quite sincere, objective reality pushed them, unintentionally, into a different position, the more awkward in that their former fellows had no adequate channels to express their views and thus influence their rulers.[3]

On the whole, society continued to be conceived by the majority of its members as basically stratified or hierarchically differentiated. The already mentioned sample of 1967 was addressed several questions concerning this issue. The question whether, in Czechoslovak society, social differences do exist

[1] Stanislaw Ossowski, *Class Structure in the Social Consciousness* (London, 1969) pp. 185–6.

[2] Ralf Dahrendorf, *Class and Class Conflict in Industrial Society* (London, 1967) p. 284.

[3] What kind of crisis this development can bring about was revealed in Poland at the close of 1970.

was answered by 74·9 per cent in the affirmative, and by only 9·5 per cent in the negative. The question whether classes or strata existed was answered by 56·5 per cent in the affirmative; 17·2 per cent denied this kind of differentiation.[1] Answers to more detailed and complex questions were analysed and distributed into seven groups. Of these, four, totalling 44 per cent of the sample, were basically of a dichotomic type: mass and élite; one of a more complex hierarchical model received 20 per cent, and one of non-hierarchical concept, 25 per cent; the official concept of the three harmoniously co-operating social groups (workers, co-operative farmers and intelligentisa) was held by only 11 per cent of the respondents.

As an illustration of our former reasoning on the limited effects of social mobility of workers to higher positions on the vertical scales further assessment of the survey is of particular importance. Dichotomic apperception of the society was more strongly represented among manual workers, whereas the official view was slightly more represented among non-manual employees.[2]

The different attitudes of these two groups of population, workers and other employees, were conspicuous on the occasions of festivals and meetings in which participation was considered to be evidence of loyalty to the régime, such as 1 May parades, Soviet Revolution celebrations, public greetings of allied visiting statesmen, political mass rallies, voluntary working brigades, etc. On all these occasions the participation of workers was usually much lower than that of white-collar employees; among these in turn the higher the position in administration or profession, the higher usually was the turnout. This was because they were either more sympathetic to or more dependent of the new establishment which provided them with better posts and therefore they had more to lose. Because of their more responsible posts, their loyalty was also more closely scrutinised. Anyhow people in higher positions behaved more in accordance with the officially designed pattern of behaviour. This was, as mentioned earlier, one additional means to attain greater security.

[1] Bohumil Jungmann, 'Sebehodnocení a sebeidentifikace', in *Československá společnost*, p. 365.
[2] Ibid. p. 373.

No wonder, that with the exception of co-operative farmers and private peasants (who together constituted, in the middle of the sixties, slightly more than 10 per cent of the population) all became virtually state, or rather Party employees because, as noted earlier, in every enterprise and institution it was up to the Party official charged with cadre policy to decide whether an individual could, for political and ideological reasons, be employed or not.[1] Thus the socialisation of the means of production provided the supreme holder of power with additional means of compulsion reaching far beyond the economic sphere but using this sphere as a channel to enforce political and ideological homogeneity within the society. This power could not possibly be challenged by the existence of several rump parties committed, by enforced agreement with the Communist leadership, to an acceptance of Communist supremacy and a limitation of membership to a few thousands – compared with a Communist Party membership of far over a million. Nor was it threatened by the churches, whose public activities were strictly limited and supervised by special officials at national and regional level.

Even the seemingly independent group of intellectuals, such as writers and artists who were not in employment (about 3,000 persons in the late sixties), felt the full effect of the above-mentioned principle because of the state monopoly of the means of public performance, publishing houses, theatres, etc. All persons in these professions had to be organised in officially supervised bodies. If they were not willing to be so organised they were obliged to take on another job. No able-bodied and mentally healthy man below 60 could live without any acknowledged employment. To live from other sources of income was a legal offence of parasitism (§ 203 of the Penal Code).

[1] The supervisory system developed a set of secret rules devising which posts had to be filled only by Communists, how many exceptions in which employments had to be admitted and which Party organ had to decide the appointments. Until 1957 the application of these rules was left, at least on the lower level of authority, widely to the discretion of individual officials charged with cadre policy. From 1958 the rules were laid down more bindingly and the individual officials had to report all cases to the Party organ authorised by the more systematic 'Cadre rules' (kádrový pořádek) to pass the final decision. In 1958 there was also a large-scale purge of deologically unreliable elements among the employees.

All this may help to understand why, whereas the number of people controlling the means of production decreased substantially, the number of people providing the means of compulsion (as shown in Table 17) considerably increased.

On the other hand the scope of control of both the means of production and of the means of compulsion increased. In the first case (means of production) this happened only at the top level where economic planning had combined the concentration of managerial decisions with price and wage regulation. Price and wage control reduced the scope of elementary market forces which hitherto were beyond the influence of most owners.[1] In the second case, that of the means of compulsion, the enlargement was a logical corollary of reduced liberties, especially those connected with spread of dissident opinions, travelling abroad and pursuing unsupervised economic activity.

The means of compulsion were amply used especially in the early fifties, when economic, administrative and judiciary methods were combined to enforce the uniformity of political behaviour and ideological adherence (if not inwardly at least outwardly). The development of the intensity of operation of the means of compulsion in this sense can be followed only with respect to judiciary activity and with respect to the policy allowing people to travel abroad.

The number of sentences for behaviour defined as anti-state activity may be used as the basic indicator of judiciary repression (Chapter I of the Penal Code), consisting predominantly of the acts and utterances of the opposition against the politico-economic system. The level of sentences for these offences underwent substantial changes during the eighteen years for which comparable data are available (see Table 47).

It is difficult to say how far these data reflect changes in the expression of political opposition itself and how far they reflect changes in the intensity of repression. However, in view of the well-known developments of the fifties it may be reasonably

[1] There was only one possibility for private owners to master the impersonal market forces, and this was the cartel. However, this practice was not very used in Czechoslovakia. Neither the state monopolies such as tobacco, spirits and, after 1935, grain, could appreciably influence the operation of market forces. Even the rent control was eventually relaxed to enable the level of rent to be adapted to the development of construction cost.

inferred that the big changes in the number of sentences reflect shifts in the repression policy of the régime rather than changes in genuine political opposition.

Table 47

FREQUENCY OF JUDICIARY REPRESSION
(PER 10,000 OF POPULATION OF PRODUCTIVE AGE)*

	Sentences for activity against	
	The State	Socialist ownership
1951	14·7	—
1952	14·3	33·8
1953	14·9	42·9
1954	10·3	49·6
1955	7·3	52·1
1956	5·6	48·0
1957	5·6	29·2
1958	6·0	36·2
1959	5·3	27·2
1960	2·9	17·5
1961	3·7	20·5
1962	1·9	19·1
1963	1·6	18·2
1964	1·1	15·6
1965	2·0	19·0
1966	3·4	22·4
1967	3·2	25·1
1968	1·2	21·4
1969	2·0	22·4

* Men from 15 to 60, women from 15 to 55; productive age has been chosen as a substitute for adult age because there were no continuous data available for the latter.

Sources: 1958–69, CS *Statistical Yearbooks*, 1951–7, *Československé trestní právo* (Prague, 1969) vol. 2, pp. 10, 78 and 220. In the latter source the data are reproduced mainly in graphic form; therefore there may be a certain margin of error in reducing them to figures. The order of magnitude, however, can hardly be different.

This statement can be further elucidated by comparing the number of political sentences with the sentences for another offence which, although apparently of a purely economic character, nevertheless has a certain political connotation, i.e. the stealing of national property. As the prosecution for this offence very often acquired features of repression of what were labelled capitalist elements or inclinations (especially cases when the former expropriated owner tried to save something for himself of the confiscated property, which was especially the case for farmers and small shopkeepers), it was officially regarded as another means of repression of class (i.e. implicitly political) enemies.

Table 47, which reviews the number of both these types of sentence, shows quite clearly that the repressive apparat gradually relaxed after 1953 and shifted its interests from direct political repression to more economic but nonetheless politically tinged offences. Their number increased until 1955 and after that never declined so sharply as the number of prosecutions for political attitudes proper.

However, in reading Table 47 we have to be reminded that the judicial cases do not constitute all cases of repression for political or politico-economic behaviour. As the non-judiciary (i.e. administrative) means of repression, such as forceful assignment to a labour camp or a brigade, banishment from a certain locality, etc., were mainly used in the fifties, the decrease of repression in the early sixties would be still more conspicuous. The change would also be more pronounced if the changes in severity of sentences (capital punishment, length of imprisonment, property confiscation, etc.) could be taken into account. In spite of these deficiencies, however, the number of political sentences can be envisaged, *cum grano salis*, as a rough indication of the intensity of the 'cold war' and the number of the other sentences in the Table 47 as an indication of the 'class war'.

As another indicator of the changing weight of the means of compulsion, the number of exit visas can be scrutinised (Table 48). Before the war, the travelling abroad was free. In 1937 the ratio of Czechoslovak citizens who left Czechoslovakia for more than a daily sojourn (in the frontier area) was 106·2 per 1,000 population. In the first postwar years the travelling abroad almost stopped, however for factual rather than legal reasons (the life in neighbouring countries was so disrupted that travelling became unattractive). After the Communist take-over in 1948, administrative barriers diminished by half even this trifle of personal contact with foreign countries. In 1949 only 4·5 persons per 1,000 population obtained exit visas – compared with 9·5 in 1947. Then during the whole of the fifties no data were disclosed. Exit visas were reserved only for a few official visits. In the early sixties, when data are again available, the rate of exit visas per 1,000 population oscillated

Table 48

TRAVELLING ABROAD
(RATIO PER 1,000 POPULATION)

Year	To all countries	To 'capitalist' countries only
1937	106·1	(105·0)*
1947	9·5	·
1948	7·2	·
1949	4·5	·
1960	37·7	·
1961	46·2	·
1962	53·5	·
1963	47·1	·
1964	147·9	·
1965	122·9	11·9
1966	137·9	14·7
1967	167·4	21·2
1968	162·6	31·3
1969	200·9	49·6
1970	144·4	13·1

* Estimate; number of visits to Soviet Russia was negligible.

Sources: 1937–49, *Statistical Bulletin* (1950) p. 82. 1960–70, CS *Statistical Year-books*.

between 37·7 and 53·5 per year. In 1964 the ratio jumped to 147·9 and remained high above the prewar level until 1969, when it attained its apogee – 200·9 per 1,000 population. During this period the share of those allowed to travel to the West increased from a tenth to a quarter of exit permits. In 1970 a re-versed trend set in. Obtaining exit visas again became difficult.

Comparing the relative power position of people in control of the means of production and people in control of the means of compulsion we must regard the latter as the stronger. Being in charge of protecting not only the new mode of production but also the political and ideological supremacy and exclusiveness of the Communist Party, they are closely linked with its apparat, and, as is well known, succeeded for a long period in being its most powerful component. In general the relative importance of the means of compulsion seems to be the greater, the more rigidly the supremacy of the Communist Party is implemented, the more it moves to the exclusively monopolistic position.

We would like to conclude this chapter with a general observation on one particular feature of the systemic transformation, i.e. on the shift in the relationship of ownership and power. Whereas in Marx's capitalism private ownership of the means of production was supposed to be the main source of power, and the state apparat, with its position of authority was supposed to be largely dependent on the interests of the most powerful owners of the means of production, in Stalinist and post-Stalin socialism the main source of power turned out to be the position of authority within the political apparat as the supreme manager of the means of production, means of education and means of compulsion simultaneously. In analogy to Marx's basic formula demonstrating the difference between capitalism and feudalism by the differing roles of money, we may express the difference between the capitalism of his day and the Marxist–Leninist socialism of ours, with respect to the relationship of ownership and power, in the following way:

$$\text{Capitalism:} \quad O \to P \to A$$
$$\text{Socialism:} \quad A \to P \to O,$$

where O stands for ownership, P for power and A for authority. In both cases ownership is understood not in legal but in factual terms, i.e. as control of the means of production in the sense already mentioned (management, control of employment and disposal of the output). Authority is understood in the sense of legitimate power based on holding a certain position within the governmental or para-governmental apparat, and power is understood in the broad, Max Weber sense as a possibility to enforce one's own will against opposition within a certain social relationship.

(G) CLASSES AND ÉLITES

It might be inferred from what has been said in the preceding chapters that there were two basic counter moves in the restructuring of Czechoslovak society after World War II. Whereas on one side there was a considerable levelling of most components of social status, on the other hand there was, as a result of an unprecedented concentration of power at the top level, a more pronounced differentiation of power.

The levelling tendency aimed primarily at the equalisation of income and of legal working conditions.

There have been several tendencies operating in favour of income levelling. One of them lies in the changes of labour supply, i.e. in the decrease of manual labour on one side and the growing supply of qualified labour on the other. The former pushed the lower wages up and the latter salaries of non-manual employees down. Also the substitution of machine for manual work was slower than might have been expected in a country with such a fast industrial growth as Czechoslovakia.

Nevertheless, these reasons cannot fully explain the magnitude of the equalisation drive after World War II. In comparison with other countries, especially socialist ones, which were undergoing a similar development, the pace of levelling seems to have been faster in Czechoslovakia.[1] This difference might be the result of a faster exhaustion of the labour reserve in a country with a smaller proportion of peasantry. Apparently another reason was the socio-cultural climate, which was highly favourable to the concept of social equality.

Here one of the Czechoslovak socio-cultural peculiarities – the bent towards egalitarianism – coalesced with the idea of redistributive justice operating within the socialist movement. As this movement, however, was completely dominated by the Marxist–Leninist concept of socialism, with its paramount stress on production, rather than upon the distribution aspects of the socio-economic system, we might have expected an assault on

[1] See J. Večerník, in *Československá společnost*, p. 298.

the class distinctions from the point of view of the division of labour.

How much more stress Marx laid on production aspects, i.e. on the necessity of equalising the positions of all employees within the production process in order to attain, eventually, the 'free association of producers individed into masters and servants', can best be seen from his scornful rejection of the Gotha programme of the German Social Democratic Party.[1] But however Marx might have poured scorn on 'vulgar' socialists, and Engels might have derided Proudhon for his believing in this 'social phlogiston justice',[2] Marx's own terminology and argumentation very often implies value judgement based on ethical concepts of social justice.

A term such as 'exploitation', with its strong ethical connotation, which is the pivotal concept of Marx's theory of value, could not but invoke quite opposite ideas on the essence of socialism to those which he had expressed in so many polemics. Also his undisguised approval of the Paris Commune's egalitarian income policy must have evoked an impression of his concern with distributive justice. For the common man unacquainted with the intricacies of high theory there are symbols which are the most important element of the doctrine; 'abolition of exploitation' has been surely the most attractive symbol that each branch of socialism, not only the Marxist one, could envisage as the basic idea of its political programme.

Further on, as exploitation was defined by Marx as a difference between the labour value of output and the value of workers' labour power used in producing this output, the whole issue could not be practically understood otherwise than in terms of income. Thus the change of ownership has always been envisaged as a necessary precondition not only for giving the workers a greater self-assertion as integrated and unalienated beings, which implied a greater say in the conditions of their daily work, but also for enabling them to acquire a fairer, i.e. greater, share of the produced value.

In fact, however, the first, true Marxian, aim of socialisation

[1] See K. Marx, *Critique of the Gotha Programme* (London, 1933) especially p. 32.

[2] F. Engels, 'The Housing Question', in *Marx and Engels, Selected Works*, I, 625.

was found to be satisfied by abolition of the legal differences between workers and other employees and by opening to political activists among workers the access to leading posts in management and ruling apparats. The second, more Proudhonian aim developed only with respect to the structure of individual incomes (as was demonstrated in Chapter 2 D), and not with respect to the workers' share in national income, as will be shown in the next chapter; or to put it the other way round, a better position of the workers has been achieved at the expense of his white-collar counterpart and of his former employer as consumer rather than at the expense of the aggregate surplus value which was now left at the disposal of the government.

Every socialist movement which adopted Marxist theory as the basic tenet had to face a double dichotomy: first, how far to push the equalisation in the mode of production and how far in the distribution; second, whether equalisation only within the amount of variable capital, or also at the expense of surplus value. Using other labels is no solution to this problem.

In Czechoslovakia the social consciousness strongly favoured the distributive aspect of socialism. As an objective of a long-term policy, the Communists have put the main stress on the mode of production, i.e. pushed strongly on the nationalisation and confiscation measures, whereas the Social Democratic Party favoured, after having committed itself deeply to the first round of nationalisation, a regulation of income policy.[1] In the short run, the Communist Party was none the less eager to support the equalisation and higher income policy especially before 1948, when the struggle for public opinion and election support was so important. Then it was more concerned with a faster growth of surplus value.

The subsequent shift in emphasis in Communist policy can be seen from the differing concepts of the first and second monetary reforms. As a corollary to the first one, all lower incomes irrespective of economic branch were preferentially increased. In the second monetary reform stress was laid on

---

[1] The differing attitudes to the production-distribution issue can be seen from the concepts of the first five-year plan as prepared by the Communist and Social Democratic Parties respectively. For a review of the basic ideas of these plans see *Nové hospodářství*, IV (1948) pp. 1 and ff.

particular branches of national economy, such as miners and industrial workers, who were envisaged as the main bearers of the production drive and also the main power basis of the régime. However, in this respect, they have been largely preceded by the Party, security and army apparats, the growth of which was, as already said, producing countervailing effects on the otherwise simplified and equalised stratification pattern.

As will be shown in the next chapter, it was not only the extention of the means of compulsion and education which made it necessary to keep a large surplus value at the disposal of the government, but also several purely economic factors such as growing investment and chronic wastage – both significant for the socialist mode of production shaped according to the Soviet pattern.

A high rate of surplus value was made possible because the concentration of power at the top level involved also the ownership of virtually all means of production, including the exclusive control over what to produce, at what price and at what cost, and the monopoly of employment.

In this respect the situation substantially differed from that during World War II when, as in so many countries, the economy was regulated as a temporary measure only by administrative means such as production quotas, consumption ratios, and price and wage controls, but all the other economic decision-making, such as employment policy, commercial contacts and distribution of profits, was left to individual owners or managers. Private ownership enabled many independent transactions, even those which were against the rules of the controlling apparat.

In comparison with that period we may well appreciate what a tremendous additional power the government obtains under the comprehensive state ownership of the means of production. The combination of highly concentrated economic power with the political and ideological monopoly within a single body is just what makes this type of socialism more totalitarian than any other brand of totalitarianism which allows the ownership to be more diffuse or ideological monopoly less rigid.[1]

---

[1] This difference becomes more obvious in comparison with those one-party states which, having a less comprehensive ideology and/or less concentrated economic management, do not command such a wide range of

In this respect, concentration of power in Communist states went far beyond the unification of legislative, executive and judiciary power, far beyond the point at which the founders of Western pluralistic states have considered it necessary to check such a concentration.

How, under conditions of such a highly concentrated power on the one hand and a widespread levelling of social status on the other, can the social stratification be conceived in terms of classes or élites? Is it still possible to speak about social classes in a society where the means of production were wholly socialised? Is it possible to speak about a power élite in a country which claims to be a people's democracy or already a socialist state? Is it true that Soviet-type socialist states have substituted for the antagonistic dichotomy of capitalists and proletarians a non-antagonistic tripartite division into workers in state enterprises, workers in co-operatives and working intelligentsia? Or has another more substantial cleavage arisen within the population?

Let us turn first to the basic question of cleavage, to the basic marks of differentiation.

Not only Eastern sociologists but also Western observers have come to the conclusion that cleavage according to the relationship to the means of production (the decisive moment for the formation of classes in the Marxist sense) has become less important in a society which claims to have become socialist. Whereas the former, however, see the main reason for this in the legal form of ownership and in the decomposition of social status connected with the traditional class positions (this, of course, does not apply to all socialist states equally – Soviet Russia, especially, seems to be least affected by it), the latter realise that the importance of socio-economic differentials has become overshadowed by or made dependent on the differences in the political structure.

Frank Parkin, in summarising recently the views of prominent students of this topic concludes that the most distinctive feature of Soviet-type societies is the cleavage between the Party and

_____

means for a concerted influencing or even manipulation of the individual's behaviour.

the people, and not between social classes in the traditional sense.[1] Although correct in principle, this is a short-cut statement. It overlooks the uneven distribution of power even within the Party, especially where the Party has acquired a mass character, and what is more important it does not touch at all the mechanism by which this cleavage is made possible; or to put it the other way round, this statement does not concern the sociologically relevant characteristics of the structure in which this type of cleavage has its roots.

Raymond Aron, to whom Parkin refers, is more cautious in saying: 'Ce que la comparaison entre l'univers soviétique et le mond occidental révèle, c'est que la structure des catégories dirigeantes et non le rapport des classes détermine l'essence des régimes économico-politiques.'[2]

Although the expression 'catégories dirigeantes' is rather vague, it nevertheless pinpoints the essence of the system from which the main cleavage results, i.e. the dirigisme of social activities. It also covers well the double type of difference, that in the socio-economic and in the political sphere. Any analysis not taking into account both of these fields would miss the point, as do the traditional concepts of socialism and capitalism, which, in covering socio-economic differences only (and what is still worse, not doing so to their full relevant extent), cannot but present a partial and therefore distorted view of social reality.

Within this context, we cannot attempt to answer the theoretically most important question of how far different political systems can be combined with different socio-economic structures. We nevertheless find it expedient to make a brief comment on this issue.

First, we have to take notice that until now, in all countries where all the large-scale means of production have been socialised, this has been done as a result of a centralised dictatorial power, which not only survived this act of its main *raison d'être*, but became then (partly because of the successfully performed socialisation, partly for other independent reasons) still more comprehensive and weighty. This remained the case also in those countries which from the beginning or later on

[1] Frank Parkin, *Class Inequality and Political Order* (London, 1971) p. 138.
[2] Raymond Aron, 'Class sociale, classe politique, classe dirigeante', in *European Journal of Sociology*, I (1960) p. 276.

admitted small peasants' and even small artisans' and shop-keepers' ownership within an otherwise socialised economy. As long as the political dictatorship and centrally planned economy were preserved, private ownership of small producers could not develop into a political or economic force of its own.

Only in one country – Yugoslavia – has the dictatorship been considerably relaxed. Significantly (we do not yet dare to say whether necessarily or incidentally) this country is also the only one which, in addition to permitting private ownership by small producers, has introduced a genuine co-operative owner-ship of the majority of the socialised means of production; simultaneously, Yugoslavia has worked out a system of econo-mic operation in which the direction of central planning com-prises only the main lines of economic development, whereas other decision making is left to be done as responses to the challenges of the market forces, the spontaneous working of which is supervised and kept within admissible limits by the managerial power of the state authorities.

Unlike Yugoslavia and Poland, Czechoslovakia never has attenuated the collective ownership of the means of production, ownership, which in terms of property value has comprised, since 1960, 100 per cent of reproducible wealth and 98 per cent of agricultural land. Of the collective ownership 91 per cent of reproducible wealth and 23 per cent of agricultural land is in state ownership, whereas the rest is in co-operative owner-ship, which, however, with the sole exception of private plots in agriculture, does not bring to the producers substantial advan-tages in comparison with state ownership.

Unlike Yugoslavia, Czechoslovakia did not admit greater scope for the market forces within its centrally planned economy. Even the steps undertaken towards this aim as a part of the economic reform in 1966–8 were too rudimentary to bring about a real change of the economic system. Only in free discussion and in envisaging future prospects of a pluralistic society did Czechoslovakia in 1968 go further than Yugoslavia.

In comparison with the socialist camp the so-called capitalist world is no less variegated with regard to the respective powers of market and state authority, and to the collective and indivi-dual ownership of means of production; on the other hand, it is more variegated with regard to the different degree of concentration of political power: from its wide diffusion within the pluralistic institutions, to its concentration in a dictatorial body or person. We could, however, hardly find in those countries such a concentration of power which would involve all its three types, in Marx's terms types of domination (*Herrschaft*): the political, ideological and economic in one sole body or person. Even if all these types of domination are vested predominantly in what may be called a ruling class, they are always more or less diffused within the framework of this class.

The unification of all power in one body or person has been hitherto, with perhaps the one exception of Yugoslavia, the basic characteristic of the so-called socialist states. This is what shifts the basic cleavage within the society from the structure of ownership to the structure of management, which in its turn is not limited to the economic sphere but encompasses the whole structure of social life.

What is then in concrete terms the main dividing line? Wesolowski is right in dismissing the formalistic Stalinist concept of two classes according to the form of socialist ownership (state and co-operative), and of one intermediary stratum of working intelligentsia,[1] as missing the point of Marx's argument, which is the polarised position within the social relationship.[2] Wesolowski is, however, overlooking the polarisation of relationship to the socialised means of production, and the impact of the extreme centralisation of all power at the top level. This leads him to a quite untenable proposition, that the 'change of a capitalist society into a socialist one is connected not only with decomposition of the signs of social position of classes, but also with the decomposition of the three aspects of class domination'.[3]

This may be understandable as a normative and not as a factual statement. Wesolowski must be aware of this fact when he says in another place in the same book, envisaging the different contradictory roles within the production process in a socialist society (such as brain as against physical workers, and

[1] Significantly this concept was shared in Czechoslovakia, according to the 1967 research, by only 11 per cent of respondents. See p. 123.
[2] Wesolowski, *Třídy, vrstvy a moc*, Czech transl. (Prague, 1969) pp. 114–18.
[3] Ibid. 139, translated by the author.

leading as against subordinated workers), and concludes,[1] in a significant again rather postulative way. 'The development of workers' autonomy aims at the liquidation of the sharp division between "managers" and "managed" within the working process.'[2]

In this single statement not developed in the rest of his work, Wesolowski touches the central nerve of the dichotomy which is at the bottom of social cleavage within the socialist society in question, namely between managers on one side and what we may briefly call producers, i.e. producers of goods and services,[3] on the other. This dichotomy fulfils conditions of an antagonistic class relationship, because it is drawn, to use again Wesolowski's interpretation of Marx's concept, between those who are 'in control of the means of production, of the working process and of the product of the work',[4] and those who 'allow themselves to be hired for work, which means that they renounce control of their working activity'.[5]

It is irrelevant for the dichotomic character of the relationship whether the supervisory position is inherited or not, or whether the subordinates agree with this division of roles or not, and whether they are aware or not of the contradictory positions. The first point is a matter of access to the class, which unlike estate or caste is not necessarily hereditary. The other point is a question of class consciousness, or as Marx put in his heavy style the class 'für sich' and the class 'an sich'. Also the extent of possible unearned income does not constitute the substance of that dichotomy although it can accentuate it very sharply.

With respect to the already mentioned more intensive use of means of non-economic domination, we may, perhaps, conceive the gist of the class division as the contradiction within the range of disposition and control of all those means which can affect anybody's life in its most essential aspects. This extends

[1] Ibid. p. 120.   [2] Ibid. p. 123.

[3] It is difficult to find a convenient term for those 'managed' with sufficient coverage of all working people outside the managerial class. After having envisaged such terms as 'operators', 'executioners' and 'taskful-fillers', the author found it best to use the most simple expression 'producers' which, however, has to be understood in the broadest sense, i.e. producers of any kind of services with the exception of managerial ones. The author is indebted to Professor Ionescu for a helpful discussion on this issue.

[4] Ibid. p. 19.   [5] Ibid. p. 29.

the concept of class relationship beyond the socio-economic sphere.

But let us stay for a while with the socio-economic relationship. As long as there is no genuine co-operative ownership as in Yugoslavia, or a large sector of small private producers as in Poland and Yugoslavia, the division of the society into a managerial class and a class of producers encompasses, in its socio-economic aspects, the whole society. It may be more or less graded as is military organisation, but the basic dichotomy between rulers and ruled is distinct.[1]

A certain gradation was always corollary to any type of polarisation or dichotomy. The efficiency of political, and to a large extent also ideological, leadership is highly dependent on it. Within the development of modern industrial and financial organisation the hierarchisation of management also became more important in the economy; actual control of most modern means of production requiring a large number of workers with different degrees of specialisation and responsibility cannot but be hierarchised. It is only the intensity of this hierarchisation which can be shaped differently.[2]

In 1967 Czechoslovakia we have identified slightly above 200,000 people who were entrusted with actual control of the means of production.[3] The discretionary power of most of them was of course very limited. Their decision making was comparatively free only to the extent of finding out the most suitable means to fulfil the targets put before them by higher authorities. The real decision making on the extent and variety of production was confined to a small number of top planners, who in their turn had to submit their decisions for the approval of the highest political authority. The latter was, in reality, wielding the supreme economic power as well.

Fulfilment of economic plans is of course only one, albeit

[1] It is significant that the view of a basically dichotomously structured society was held by the majority of the Czechoslovak sample asked for opinion on this issue in autumn 1967 (see p. 123).

[2] In this direction also most of the economic liberalisation may be actualised. Its impact can only gradualise but not abolish the main cleavage within the economic relationship, let alone attenuate the power structure in other respects. In this sense economic liberalisation amounts to nothing more than decartelisation or to similar anti-trust measures in the West.

[3] See Table 45 and p. 111.

essential, duty of socialist citizens. Their other important duty is ideological conformity and readiness to follow any Party and government appeal for social action.

The economic rewards have to be adapted to this aim, and means of education have to be adequately developed and strictly supervised. Unlike so often in the West, education is not conceived as just a supply of specialist services, from which on the highest level the student, as a consumer, is free to choose without regard to his possible further career – but as a training activity for a particular vocation which those who were admitted to benefit from it have to accept, together with its unilaterally ideological guidance without reservation. This of course implies a more or less detailed planning of curricula by central authorities. Finally where economic inducement and education measures fail, means of compulsion have to intervene, the more swiftly and resolutely the more the failure has been of an ideological nature.

Understandably such a system of extended social management in combination with a highly centralised economy (not only by means of ownership but also of the planning system) necessitates, as already demonstrated, a higher number of persons in control of the centralised means of education and compulsion than of means of production.

In the absence of direct data on the managerial class, outside the economic sphere, we have to base our estimates on the already frequently mentioned representative data of the 1967 research. Taking into account persons which this research classified as authority holders on the level of organisations (15·4 per cent of the sample which represents the sum of the heads of households)[1] we can assume that the whole managerial class comprised 650–700,000 active persons, i.e. about 10 per cent of the working population (labour force). Of this 10 per cent, according to our comprehensive list of persons in direct control of the means of production (see Table 45), economic managers comprised less than one-third.

What is now the relationship between the managerial class as conceived above and the power élite, or as Wesolowski puts it with respect to the socialist order in question, the political

[1] See pp. 117–18.

leadership?[1] Wesolowski's terminological preference cannot be dismissed as only apologetical semantics.[2] It may be understood as reflecting the shift from a differentiated power structure to a uniform one where all an individual's power emanates from his position within the political hierarchy.

In Czechoslovakia this change in the power structure occurred gradually after 1948. The independent economic power of individuals was broken by successive nationalisation and collectivisation measures and by monetary reform in 1953; independent ideological power, which after the crushing of non-Communist parties in February 1948 was especially that of the Catholic Church (this was of paramount importance mainly in Slovakia), was broken by administrative and punitive measures in 1949–51, when religious orders were dissolved, Church administration and pastoral activity of clergy put under state control and priests who had not taken the oath of allegiance to the government were dismissed or, in cases of recalcitrance, imprisoned. These measures affected most bishops, whose offices were left vacant.

Only then did the real power structure become a uniform one, i.e. vested in and centred around the Communist Party and graded according its hierarchy as a spine. Centralised leadership and administration and strict discipline became the main prerequisites of keeping all personnel and technical means of executive power under firm command.

Even such a tight power structure, however, does not exclude competition between people with different professional backgrounds to attain greater power within or through the Party apparat. The outcome of this competition may even result in certain changes within the power élite, i.e. different professional groups of the élite may become more influential within the state in different periods of development. It might even happen that some social groups, exposed to excessive pressure in particu-

---

[1] Wesolowski, ibid. 136.

[2] Although earlier (p. 61) Wesolowski conceived the difference between class and élite by deriving the former from the economic and the latter from the political system, he nevertheless prefers, for a socialist society, a term in which politics is explicitly mentioned; as he puts in p. 136, he wants to stress the special marks and composition of the leading group (i.e. the materialisation of mass interests and proletarian origin).

lar circumstances, expressed their dissent by means of strikes, refusal of deliveries or something similar.

These phenomena are often regarded as proof of the thesis that no totalitarian system can be so rigid as not to allow some scope for social conflict and possibly also change. This is surely true. As every totalitarianism is theoretically based on a utopian concept which as a rule wants to change a spontaneous living organism into a programmed organism or rather mechanism (the intensity of wanted change depends on the comprehensiveness of the totalitarian concept), this endeavour can be successful only up to a point. Success depends (*a*) on the extent of the means at the disposal of the power centre and (*b*) on the intelligence and dexterity of the decision makers, i.e. whether they are ready to compromise with unalterable human needs and interests.

Even after a totalitarian system has been so successful as to avoid for long periods any overt clashes such as strikes and similar kinds of effective dissent, as was the case of Czechoslovakia in 1953–67, there was nevertheless scope for certain changes within the élite structure.

Looking back to the development of Czechoslovak society since World War II we might discern a certain movement within the power élite, which after 1948 became exclusively an élite within the Communist Party.

In the short period of pluralistic constellation of power,[1] i.e. from May 1945 to February 1948, we may identify about ten professional groups who might be described as components of the power élite; civil servants, managers, private entrepreneurs, military personnel, police, party officials, trade union officials, clergymen (especially in Slovakia), technical experts and intellectuals.[2]

[1] For an explanation of this term within the context of parameters of politico-economic systems see my contribution to the discussion on *Cultural Streams in Systematics*, VIII (1970) p. 45.

[2] Intellecturals are here understood as that part of the intelligentsia who are primarily active as researchers, scientists, university teachers, writers, artists, etc. In this sense intellectuals are in most cases identical with cultural intelligentsia but form only a fraction of it. To a lesser extent technical intelligentsia also fall into this group. On the other hand, technical experts are here understood as people (mainly of technical intelligentsia but partly also belonging to cultural intelligentsia as in the case of economists and

After 1948, private enterpreneurs and clergymen disappeared from the élite structure, being not, as a matter of principle, eligible for membership of the Communist Party. Of all the other groups the Party officials became most important and every other professional group had within the Party apparat a corresponding section. Party officials had also the technical means at their disposal for playing the really leading role in the state.

However, from about 1950 the police officials, because of their direct link with the corresponding authorities in the Soviet Union, acquired a largely independent position which in many concrete instances was even superior to that of the Party officials. The power of the military apparat grew simultaneously apparently because of tension between the world power blocs. It may be inferred that during the early fifties the party, the police and the military apparats provided the core of the power élite in the state, with the police being the strongest among them.

In the second half of the decade however, with a recession of international tension and also with respect to personal changes in army leadership (especially the ousting of the former President Gottwald's son-in-law, Čepička, from the post of minister), the army became less powerful. The same, perhaps, to a larger extent, happened with the police, as a result of a weakening of police power in Soviet Russia.

Thus the party apparat regained its exclusive leading position. The First Secretary of the Party, who was at the same time the head of state (president), controlled not only the party and state apparats, but also contacts with the Kremlin, which thus could not be circumvented by other channels such as formerly had been the case with the police apparat. This situation continued into the early sixties, when as a result of some apparent

---

lawyers) who do not belong to any other profession in the list but nevertheless have a relevant say in these professions as advisers. There might be, of course, some intermingling amongst these groups, but the main vocational character depends on the basic function and attitude of the person concerned.

Whereas in defining intelligentsia we had to use as the main criterion, in order to make this concept quantifiable, the degree of education, in this analysis we focus our attention on professions without regard to whether the people involved attained a certain degree of education or not, and consider only those people of those professions who are in a certain position of power, be it in the sense of authority or influence.

economic difficulties which will be dealt with in the next chapter the managers and technical experts, especially economists, began to play a more important role within the power élite.

From about the early sixties the intellectuals, who of all the élite groups were most aware of humanitarian values (which were so downtrodden during the fifties), took the initiative in the movement towards rehabilitation of these values. This involved both personal rehabilitation of the victims of pre-fabricated trials, and institutional safeguards for strict legality in the future and greater scope for intellectual freedom.

The technical intelligentsia, seeing better prospects for its self-assertion in greater personal freedom and in the more efficiency-minded economy, joined in. The need for change, until then voiced only occasionally and usually outside the power élite, began to be felt within the élite structure. It eventually broke out into a palace revolt within the Politbureau at the turn of 1967–8, resulting in personnel changes in the party apparat.

During 1968–9 the position of individual professional groups within the power élite was once more equal. Party officials gave up a little of their previous monopoly and conceded a certain scope for independent activity to the representatives of other professional groups such as writers, scientists, mass media operators, technical experts and finally trade union representatives, within the party. Although there was no reversion to the immediate postwar period (the movement outside the Communist Party was comparatively limited and did not go, as a rule, beyond the postulates voiced within the Communist Party itself) it nevertheless provided ample opportunity for the broadening of the power élite, both in qualitative and quantitative terms.

It is worth while mentioning that the new enlarged and more equal élite pattern survived the Soviet military intervention for a whole year, and then the pattern of the early sixties was reintroduced only gradually. In view of what had happened on other similar occasions, e.g. also after the Communist take-over in 1948, there seems to be a time-lag between a military intervention or *coup d'état* and the virtual restructing of élites.

*

After having discovered, with respect to the functional structure[1] of the society, the main lines of social cleavage, and after having analysed both the class and élite aspects of this cleavage, we may return to Parkin's thesis and reassess the relevance of Party membership.

It is a well-known fact that Czechoslovakia has in relation to the whole population the largest Party membership of all Communist countries. This of course is not because its power élite is more numerous or the power more diffuse than in other Soviet-type societies. It is a result of the particular tactics of the Czechoslovak Communist Party during the struggle for power in the late forties. In appreciation of the favourable circumstances for a social change on socialist lines and of the pro-Soviet sympathies which distinguished Czechoslovakia from other European countries (see p. 2), the Communist Party of Czechoslovakia endeavoured to acquire the widest possible membership with a fair hope for the gradual re-education of those who were fit for it.

This policy was intensified in the aftermath of the February takeover in 1948. Rival political parties had to be destroyed not only through oppressive measures taken against their leaders but also through the large recruitment to the Communist Party. Thus, from the end of February to the end of August 1948, the Communist Party membership increased from 1,409,661 to 2,674,838.[2] It seemed to be more expedient to incorporate the politically minded population into the Communist Party where they could be re-educated than to leave them outside the Party where the ideological control of them could not be so intensive. There was always ample opportunity to get rid of those who would not yield, by means of periodical purges. The result of these successive purges brought the membership down to 1,385,610 in the spring of 1954.[3]

From the viewpoint of those who in those extraordinary circumstances entered the Communist Party, the reasons may have been mainly of two types. There were ambitious people

---

[1] We use the word 'functional' in the common-sense meaning and not in the sociologists' partisan connotation (functionalist as against conflict theory concepts).

[2] *Dějiny Československa v datech*, p. 379.

[3] *Protokol X. řádného sjezdu KSČ* (Prague, 1954) p. 90.

who did not want to lose the position which they had already acquired within the power élite, and they knew that only by joining the Communist Party might they be allowed either to keep their posts or to acquire, in due time, a substitute for them. The other reason may have been just the simple need for social security and for better prospects for their children. We have dealt with this particular aspect of Party membership in Chapter 2 (E). We have also indicated that even in 1967 the Party membership consisted mainly of heads of households, i.e. fathers of families, whereas among the younger population and unattached individuals Party membership was negligible.

The sociological research on which these conclusions are based had also revealed that there were a substantial number of Communists without power positions, and, on the other hand, many non-Communists in higher brackets of the power hierarchy. Can we infer from this that, because the division of power is not strictly on Party membership lines, the basic cleavage is not between Party and non-Party members? This conclusion would surely be preposterous. The figures remind us only that we are faced with a more complicated relationship than may be inferred from the dividing line between Party and non-Party members.

From what we have said on the recruitment of Party members, we realise that the Party had, especially during the early fifties, a lot of half-hearted members[1] kept in obedience by the general atmosphere of fear and insecurity. The Party had also, especially in the older generation of workers, many of those who were uninterested in active politics and did not compete for position within the power hierarchy.

On the other hand the Communist Party was able to acquire a certain support or co-operation outside the Party membership. This was a very intricate relationship carried on through different channels, such as, especially, the dependence of leaders of puppet political parties (remnants of parties destroyed after February 1948) on the Communist leadership, and secret collaboration with the security apparat.

Thus, although Party membership was one of the basic conditions for promotion within the power hierarchy it was not

[1] The so-called 'radishes' (i.e. red from without and white within) in popular language.

a sufficient condition. Within the Party, only the 'activists', i.e. those who showed a determined effort to enforce the Party line wherever they were asked to do so had the best prospects of promotion.

During the most decisive period of building socialist society in Czechoslovakia, i.e. in the first five years after 1948, only the Party-line zealots (the stress was laid on the Party line of the time being not on Communist ideology as such) could acquire or keep decisive positions within the Party and state apparats. Only they could command the means of compulsion, the means of education and at the top level the means of production. As time went on, the zealotism became routine, changes in the Party line more frequent and the difference between commanded (administrative) and genuine (ideological) zealotism became obvious. Party zeal could under certain circumstances make good the lack of the right class origin or former membership of another Party. On the other hand faithful co-operation from beyond Party lines could also bring a reward. Here, however, the distinction should be made between reward in terms of real power, i.e. the possibility of deciding issues against the will of others and especially deciding the fate of others, and material advantages only.

Real power, especially decision making on others, such as their non-manual employment, access to higher education, rewards in money or in kind, access to travelling abroad, etc., was always at the top level, reserved for Communists only. Non-Communist collaborators could only acquire easier access to those rationed benefits and up to a point ease it also for their own helpers or relatives. Only badly needed unreplaceable technical experts could be dealt with in a preferential way without fulfilling the political prerequisites; in competition with Party members working in their field, however, they had, as a rule, to take on a less responsible job.

Speaking on decision making we have also to make a distinction between decisions on aims and decisions on means. The former were always reserved for the top organs of the Party. Only the latter were left over to the lower echelons of the apparat, whether Party or government, or possibly to the non-Party technical experts.

In this respect the structure of the whole society may be

equated to that of an army. The decision making is graded in a similar way as between general staff, individual generals, officers and N.C.O.s. There is, nevertheless, a substantial difference between the military and the Communist hierarchy. The latter is strongly conditioned by a heavy ideological commitment. Even the decision making on the means had to be done according to the ideological tenets. When for instance agricultural output was to be put up or consumer services developed or new technology introduced, neither private initiative nor contacts with abroad could be developed more fully without a special decision of the top leaders on this particular measure.

As we have already indicated, the 1968 developments broadened the power élite not only with respect to individual professions but also with respect to the Party membership. Greater numbers of Party members acquired greater say in the decision making, and ideological considerations independent of the approved opinion from above started to play an important role. Virtually, it was not the Party hegemony but the hegemony of the ruling minority within the Party which was put to question.[1]

Had the economic reform materialised, the socio-economic differentials as such might have regained some of their former importance.

Summing up all these qualifications we can describe the most relevant dividing line within the contemporary Czechoslovak society in the following way.

The basic functional division is between managers and producers. As the former have, in a strictly hierarchised pattern, the exclusive control of the means of production, education and compulsion, whereas the latter are hired only to operate them, the basic characteristics of class relationship is fulfilled.

As in every society, the power is not evenly distributed among the ruling class. Only a part of it – those vested with decision

---

[1] Again this broadening of the strata with political influence did not go so far as to enable the simulating Communists ('radishes'), who survived the subsequent purges in the Party to gain some influence. Those who sought in Party membership social security were too cautious to take any risk in the forthcoming struggle, the outcome of which was far from certain.

making on most relevant issues – can be described as the power élite. The difference between the power élite and the management class as a whole is the more conspicuous, the more the supreme power is centralised. The extent and professional composition of the power élite varies with the changes in the degree of this centralisation and with the intensity of its grip (dictatorship).

Access to the management class in general and to the power élite in particular depends primarily on the political attitudes of the persons concerned. Only when it is absolutely necessary, e.g. in medicine and technology, is the specialist qualification (education and experience) the decisive factor.

The relative importance of political qualification increases with the level of authority. Thus it plays a much more important role in the access to the power élite than to lower managerial posts both in economic and non-economic spheres. Non-Communists can attain positions within the power élite only when they are determined and faithful collaborators of the régime or, exceptionally, when they command exclusive technical knowhow which has top priority among the politically determined objectives. The Communists themselves, if they want to assume or to keep their posts within the power élite, have to show a resolute determination in pursuit of the Party line of the time.

According to the statistical evidence and research results quoted above, we may assess, in Czechoslovakia, the proportion of Communists within the managerial class to be about three-fifths, and among the power élite to be about four-fifths, on the eve of the 1968 events. To put it the other way round, only about a quarter of the Communist membership then belonged to the managerial class, and about 10 per cent to the power élite.

On the other hand, the intelligentsia appeared less successful in the power hierarchy. According to the 1967 sample, scarcely a half of persons belonging to the groups which roughly correspond to our concept of the managerial class had a higher or complete secondary education. According to the comprehensive statistics on most of the managerial personnel in the economic sector, the proportion of those with the required specialist qualification was somewhat lower. The same applies to that part of the managerial class which might be included in

the power élite (directors and deputy directors of big enterprises).

Although we have not the corresponding figures for the other
sections of the managerial class, we may suppose that a better
proportion of qualified personnel in the means of education
may be outweighed by a lower proportion of such personnel in
the means of compulsion, so that the general picture would not
be substantially different from that mentioned above. To sum
up: of the whole of the intelligentsia as a social group (1,145,000
in 1966), only about 30 per cent belong to the managerial class,
and scarcely 5 per cent to the power élite.

What is then the position and structure of the producing
class in Czechoslovak society? Comprising 90 per cent of the
gainfully active population, its relative weight in the nation
surpasses the proportion of working class in pre-war Czechoslovakia, when there was a strong 'middle-class' sector.

In 1930 the structure was approximately as follows: 57 per
cent workers, 7 per cent other employees, 30 per cent small
producers, 6 per cent capitalists (see Table 15); making allowance for the low living standard of some small producers on one
side, and of well-to-do workers' categories on the other, we may
evaluate the strength of pre-war middle-class at a good third of
the Czechoslovak population.

What happened then to this middle-class in the process of
socialisation? The answer cannot be unequivocal. With regard
to the relationship to the means of production the middle-class
has been thoroughly proletarianised. Even in farmers' co-
operatives the co-ownership of the collective property is rather
nominal.

On the other hand, with respect to most components of social
status, a larger part of the nation acquired middle-class
character.[1] This happened especially with regard to the amount
of income, consumer pattern, legal conditions of employment,

---

[1] This striking contradiction may be understandable nevertheless. Robert
Kalivoda, in pondering why the slave revolutions in antiquity were not
successful, concluded that they could not be so because the slaves could not
postulate the transformation of their own class position into that of the whole
society, but endeavoured to get rid of their own position instead. (Robert
Kalivoda, *Husitská ideologie* (Prague, 1961) p. 478). The same can be said of
proletarians. Therefore when they cannot get rid of their lack of control of

social security and to some extent also personal wealth (especially ownership of radios, television sets and washing machines, not so much with respect to housing and other consumer durables). A comprehensive school system did also, to some extent, contribute to this development.

As an illustration, changes in the income structure from employment can be reviewed. As was shown in Table 24, in 1937 only 20 per cent of income recipients were in the middle income bracket (12–24,000 Kčs per year in 1958–68 purchasing power); in 1967 this proportion increased to 47, and in 1968 to 62 per cent. The effect of levelling is similar, if family incomes are compared. Using the statistics of household accounts, we can realise the almost identical weight of middle income positions in all the three main social groups of the economically active population: workers' households 61 per cent, in employees' households 60·5 per cent and in co-operative farmers' households 57·3 per cent. Only pensioners' households lagged behind with 47·6 per cent (for more detail see Table 32).

Despite the widespread income levelling, however, there remained still in 1965 14 per cent of workers' households, 6 per cent of employees' households, 12 per cent of co-operative farmers' households and 30 per cent of pensioners' households below the equivalent of £312 per head and year (see p. 74), which may be classified as a proletarian standard.

Since according to our findings in chapter 2 (D) the current consumption pattern and ownership of many consumer durable goods is mainly dependent on the amount of income and the size of family (which in its turn is also increasingly tending to a middle-size), the development towards a middle position may be supposed in many aspects of the style of life.

The tendency towards a middle-class position in style of life is also corroborated by the analysis of social status components by age groups. The 1967 research revealed that in most components of social status the values are more centred around the middle position in younger age groups than in older ones. This

---

the means of production they try (and this may seem to them more important) to get rid of their style of life, which until then was the corollary to their fully proletarian position. On the other hand, however, they may well succeed in imposing their lack of ownership of the means of production on a wider strata of population.

is most conspicuous and also significant with the component which might be expected to depend least on age alone and which the researchers explicitly conceived of as style of life. The convergence tendency in it can be seen from Table 49.

Table 49

LIVING STYLE BY AGE GROUPS
IN PER CENT OF THE TOTAL NUMBER OF RESPONDENTS
IN EACH GROUP

	Age groups			
Style	*To 31*	*32–46*	*47–61*	*62–76*
Upper	18·5	23·2	15·7	4·3
Middle	58·0	50·1	46·2	35·3
Lower	23·5	26·7	37·1	60·4

Source: František Povolný, 'Význam věkových a generačních skupin v sociální differenciaci', in *Českoslovanská společnost*, p. 475.

Objective material prerequisites alone, however, do not fully determine social consciousness. A good deal is still accounted for by subjective factors. These may carry over residual valuations from the past or anticipate future development. Transfer of self-identification to another objective position in time is more decisive with people who, having lost their property or given up good jobs, touch on the poverty level but nevertheless try to keep, as far as possible, the middle-class style of life. They surely do not identify themselves with the lower class. Similarly people aspiring to better jobs or to higher positions often identify themselves with their future environment.

All this has to be borne in mind in view of the particular vertical social mobility which within eight years brought more than 300,000 workers in to the social group of non-manual employees, in most cases to posts on the managerial level. On the other hand about 400,000 former non-manual employees, professionals and entrepreneurs were made manual workers. Whereas the former adapted themselves gradually to the middle-class standards and behaviour, the latter did not lose these by their social decline.[1] The enhanced vertical mobility has thus contributed also towards the increase of what may be called middle-class behaviour in the society.

On the other hand, even within such an enhanced concentration around the average, some differentials remain significant. They are due to the environmental and technological factors rather than to the differences in income and wealth. Such, in the first place, is the difference between the basically rural vocations such as agriculture and forestry on one side and the predominantly urban (i.e. all other vocations) on the other. Further difference of that kind is the difference between manual and non-manual types of work.

The difference between agriculture and other branches of economy is combined with the different relationship to the means of production or rather to the disposition of products within agriculture. Of the labour force predominantly engaged in agriculture there were in 1968 28 per cent wage earners, 59 per cent co-operative farmers and 13 per cent individual farmers. Of the latter, however, about two-thirds were women, the husbands of whom worked elsewhere.

This differentiation makes the peasantry a not quite coherent group. Although the particular environment and type of work makes of the people engaged in agriculture a distinct section within the larger group of manual workers, their different degree of disposal over their products has some relevance. The proportion of real individual farmers (i.e. gaining their livelihood mainly from agriculture) being negligible, it is the difference between wage earners and co-operative farmers which matters. Their differing position does not lie so much in the different type of collective ownership as such (co-operative as against state ownership) as in the provision that co-operative farmers get a part of their income from the co-operative in kind and in addition may operate their private plots, which makes them within the limits of their productive capacity less dependent on the state operated market.[2]

---

[1] Despite the official claim that the workers are the ruling class, to cease to be worker is generally accepted as a promotion and to become a worker, even if it is motivated as re-education measure, as a demotion.

[2] According to a private estimate the income (in money and in kind) from private plots was about a third of the total personal income of co-operative

The other important distinction is that between manual and non-manual wage earners. The 1967 research has revealed that in the social consciousness this dichotomy was still alive, although substantially altered by the progressing decomposition of other elements of social status, traditionally connected with this difference. Although many workers try to imitate the middle-class way of life, for which they have ample opportunities especially in higher income brackets, they often continue to be strongly aware of their distinction from non-manual workers, whom they sometimes see as allies or helpers of the managers, their real antipodes within the working process.[1] On the other hand, the large-scale transfer of white-collar workers to manual labour helped somewhat to overcome this barrier.

In general, workers seem to have realised that it is not so much individual personal relationships as the impersonal relationship determined by the whole system which makes their position thoroughly dependent. To put it the other way round, they do realise that although their working and security conditions have been put on the same legal basis as those of the non-manual employees (see p. 41), they are still wage earners and not co-owners of the socialised property which remains in the control of people other than themselves.

As revealed by statistics, manual workers remain the bulwark of the class of producers. Only those who have acquired the non-manual employee status (about 10 per cent) may have entered into the class of managers. There they have taken over control not only of the means of production but also the means of compulsion and of the cadre policy in the means of education. The channel for this takeover was provided exclusively by the Communist Party. There were of course some failures: some workers promoted to managerial posts realised that they did not

---

farmers in the early sixties (*Socilání struktura socialistické společnosti* ed. P. Machonin (Prague, 1966) p. 487). Since then, however, this share seems to have diminished.

[1] In this context we have to bear in mind that non-manual employees are the only social group which is substantially touched by the division into classes. With the exception of chairman of farmers' co-operatives all managers are employees, even those of worker origin. Not all employees, however, are managers. The whole managerial class comprises about one-third of the total of non-manual employees.

meet the demands of their jobs (the Party had in such cases the tendency to provide the workers' managers with the support of technical experts, even from outside the Party ranks) and renounced their positions, but there were others who, after having completed their vocational training, did a good job. The political zealots succeeded in overcoming their limitations by Party rhetoric and vigilance rather than by professional performance.

We have already expressed our doubts on the continuing working-class character of these representatives of the working class. It should not be forgotten, however, that they were the only workers who acquired some real power. On the other hand the institutional representatives of the working class, i.e. those in the trade unions, had a very limited influence on management. Although formally co-operating in hiring and firing workers and employees, their opinion could hardly alter decisions made by officials entrusted with the cadre policy in the factory or institution concerned.

Despite over 90 per cent of all the labour force in the state socialist sector (in 1967 over 5 million persons) were members of the united trade unions, the latter have enjoyed less real bargaining power than the 191 workers' and 508 non-manual employees' trade unions in 1936 (with a total membership of 2,219,000, i.e. only 70 per cent of the labour force).[1] The main activity of the present trade unions consists in the administration of social welfare, health insurance and workers' recreation.

One of the main changes in the social climate in 1968 was the gradual re-emergence of trade unions as a real social power. They regained some of their independence and acquired a greater say in employment policy, which shortly before then had become concentrated in the hands of professional managers (as long as they were reliable Party members) instead of the cadre officials. Thus management and representatives of producers started to reflect more truly the actual state of the dichotomic society. On the other hand workers' councils, the campaign on behalf of which was launched in the middle of 1968, ought to have diminished this dichotomy by superimposing on the managers a representative body of producers. This measure was

---

[1] CS *Statistical Yearbook* (1938) p. 242.

intended as the most important step in attenuating the antago-
nist class character which developed during the fifties and which
has been envisaged by many reformers as incompatible with
the concept of a true socialism.

CHAPTER THREE

Plan and Market
Relevance of Economic Factors

(A) BIRTH AND BASIC PROBLEMS OF THE COMMAND ECONOMY

In the preceding chapter we have touched several times on the changes in the economic system. We did it, however, cursorily and incidentally, only as far as it seemed necessary for a better understanding of changes in the social stratification. Now we have to deal with this particular topic in some detail in order to elucidate the impact of the economic issues, especially of plan/market dichotomy, on social development at large and on the process of liberalisation and decentralisation in the late sixties in particular.

It is a well-known fact that Czechoslovakia embarked on the road of planned economy in 1946 when preparing her first two-year plan for 1947–8. However, this was a rudimentary plan encompassing only investment and several dozen production targets in physical terms. More comprehensive planning was introduced only gradually after 1948.

It is significant for the situation after the war that both the two-year plan and the first five-year plan (1949–53) were prepared on party rather than government lines. Whereas in the two-year plan the initiative was fully with the Communists, for the five-year plan, Communist and Social Democratic Parties submitted their own versions, differing widely in scope, method and targets.

The Social Democratic draft put stress on global planning, using national accounting techniques as the main safeguard of harmonious development, kept the amount of net investment below 15 per cent of the planned national income and made the rate of growth dependent mainly on the possible labour force, fuel and energy supply. No planned reorientation of production was envisaged; its structure had to develop according to the spontaneous inter-industrial relationships within the planned rate of growth and income policy affecting consumer demand.

The Communist draft was concerned with a substantial reorientation of the economy, with the faster rate of growth and with considerably higher investment, the structure of which had to be shifted to the benefit of heavy engineering and other means of production. Methodologically, the Communist draft continued to rely primarily on the individual physical targets, the number of which were to be greatly increased and the interrelation of which was to be assured by a system of material balances.

After a period of negotiation on the party and government (planning authorities) level, a compromise was reached, reflecting the approximate respective bargaining strength of the parties involved. (The Czech National Socialist Party elaborated only a programmatic proclamation and the Czech People's and Slovak Democratic Parties, being suspicious of economic planning as such, did not submit any programme at all.)

Meanwhile, however, the so-called 'February events' in 1948 occurred and the Communists, having done away with the political opposition, took over their full responsibility for further economic development. The purged Central Planning Committee not only returned to the original Communist draft but from 1951 even adopted its still more radical version, i.e. with a higher quota of investment and with still more stress on heavy industry, especially engineering, which now was to help to build the economic strength of the whole Soviet-led bloc.

The scope of targets, planned in physical units, increased and the State Planning Office took over, from 1949, the task of centrally fixing all wholesale and virtually also retail prices. On the other hand, the work on the national accounting system which – coupled with an appropriate accounting system in enterprises – made good headway in 1949, was interrupted in 1950. It happened mainly because of distrust of the non-party experts who might have gained too much insight into the key spots of the economy. Later on the newly improved and well functioning double entry accounting system was superseded by a less coherent Soviet system ('khozraschot') which abolished the hardly established links between enterprise and national accountancy.

The principle widely observed until then, that in all balances (both in physical and monetary terms) reserves for emergency use should be kept, was rejected as a Trotskyist–Bukharinist deviation and the true Stalinist mobilising idea of balances – where the needs exceed the resources – was accepted as a rule. Investment targets were continuously put beyond the level of construction capacity and beyond the real savings. Targets in industries which became top priorities such as mining, machinery, especially heavy engineering, building material, etc., were strained to the utmost. Personnel from supposedly less essential jobs such as in consumer services were mobilised for heavy industry. Mining and quarrying was, to a large extent, manned by forced labour.

Gradually the system of planned targets assumed almost unmanageable proportions. The number of individual targets in physical units grew from about 200 in 1948 to about 2,000 in 1950 and to about 15,000 in the late fifties. Although this was only 1 per cent of commodities within the Czechoslovak economy the balancing of so many items became more and more difficult. The Leontiev's input/output matrix was rejected as a bourgeois pseudo-scientific concept until the early sixties. Mutual relations among individual targets were seen primarily as technical relations, without due respect to the possible socio-economic dimensions. Financial problems were viewed as secondary and had to be solved in a way guaranteeing success of the decisions made by production experts.

The value of gross production in constant prices was conceived as the main complex production target in industry, construction and agriculture. Labour productivity indicators were also based on it. As the fulfilment of the gross production targets reflected not only the value added but also the magnitude of inter-industrial deliveries (input of other enterprises increased automatically the value of production), the fulfilment of global plans depended not only on the real achievements but on the ability of individual management to assure enough co-operation among individual factories. The magnitude of the upward bias of these indicators can be seen from the difference of lines 7 and 9 in Table 50.[1]

A more serious problem for the management was the fulfilment of individual targets in physical units. Because of them other production within the branch was often neglected.

The expanding investment and production had to be financed to a large extent by expansion of credit beyond the savings ratio both in the private and public sectors. After four years, the inflationary pressure, which could be only partly absorbed by the free market (basic consumer goods were rationed until 1953), attained such proportions that a complex monetary reform, already the second after the war, had to be undertaken. What a drastic repudiation of the population's financial claims it constituted, has already been shown in chapter 1 (C), especially in Table 10.[2]

External trade was reorientated towards the East, the economic argument being that the socialist countries with a planned economy are not subject to market fluctuation and therefore can provide more secure long-term prospects for production orientation.

The Soviet–Yugoslav split which occurred in 1948 and which resulted in a complete breakdown of economic relations and therefore mutual deliveries, revealed the limits of such reasoning. The Soviet–Chinese split in 1960–1 had similarly adverse

[1] Based on 1948, the official index of industrial production attained 515 points in 1966, whereas the index computed from national income by industrial origin in constant prices (in our opinion the most plausible index which can be computed from other official sources) attained in the same year only 337 points. This certainly is not a negligible upward bias, allegedly of 1 per cent magnitude as Goldman–Kouba suppose in their otherwise extremely valuable analysis (*Hospodářský růst v ČSSR* 2nd ed. (Prague, 1969) p. 64). Paradoxically they base their assumption on J. G. Staller's index, which as can be seen from our Table 50 only slightly differs from the index computed from the net industrial production in national income series.

[2] Although disastrous for consumers, the monetary reform of 1953 was a considerable help to the planners. It made a 'tabula rasa' for the future planning which was then unhampered by previously accumulated assets. As in February 1948 the Communists destroyed the political power of their former coalition partners, so in June 1953 they destroyed the last remaining uncontrolled economic strength of individuals, whether friends or foes. Since collectivisation of agriculture made a fast progress in the subsequent years, no excuse because of internal capitalist influences on the economy could be called for if something went wrong with the economic plan.

effects on production orientated to long-term deliveries among the Communist states.

Meanwhile, the competitive position of Czechoslovakia in foreign markets was made more difficult by the revaluation of ner currency performed in connection with the monetary reform on 1 June 1953. With respect to the official exchange ratio to one U.S. dollar, the revaluation was by 39 per cent. From then on vital exports had often to be subsidised, even if the export goods were not, as a matter of principle, taxed by the turnover tax. On the other hand, the advantages of cheaper imports were to a considerable extent invalidated by several factors such as dependence on low-grade iron ore from Soviet Russia, the embargo on some badly needed materials from the West, and inducement by the plan's indicators (gross output) to use raw material lavishly, which for industrial use had mostly to be imported.

Special problems arose from the planning of agricultural production. Here weather had to be acknowledged as a more unstable element than external relationships. Nevertheless it was supposed that its vagaries could be overcome by long-term policy and that productivity especially could be increased by the collective, factory-like mode of production. However, productivity increased considerably only with respect to the labour force engaged (which was gradually replaced by machine work on an ascending scale), and not with respect to the area under cultivation.

During the fifties agriculture was deprived of many good and dedicated farmers, mostly owners of medium sized or even small farms (15–20 hectares), who, after having served a sentence for opposing collectivisation, were not allowed to return to their vocation. On the other hand the staff of the state tractor stations who had to provide the co-operatives with mechanised labour were not as a rule too enthusiastic about their work. This resulted in considerable neglect of maintenance of machines. State tractor stations had to be continuously subsidised until they were handed over to the co-operatives (gradually from 1960). In 1960 also, more incentive prices for state deliveries were introduced. Fertilisers were provided in adequate supply only from the middle sixties. Thus it happened that only in 1957 did the agricultural output per hectare attain the 1936 level and only in 1963 did productivity per hectare begin to increase to above the prewar level.[1]

Despite all the obvious inadequacies in handling economic reality, planning was proclaimed to be a law of socialism, a law in the objective sense of natural laws. The economy was supposed to behave according to the planners' orders, who decided as the volume of production so the prices.

The spontaneous forces of individual economic units, regulating through demand and supply the extent and variety of production, were frowned upon as remnants of capitalism and the main source of economic disturbances. The operation of market forces was reduced to contact with households and non-socialist states; nevertheless for other economic transactions the operation of the market was replaced from 1950 by the obligatory contracts which all enterprises and organisations of the socialist sector, including obligatory agricultural deliveries, had to agree upon. It was understood that for the planned targets which more often than not resulted from the summations of claims of other industries the corresponding sales had to be assured. To this end, some outward paraphernalia of the market were found convenient.

Theoretically the contracting covered, in monetary value, about 70 per cent of all economic transactions in goods and material services.[2] Even the external trade was involved, because the state monopoly import and export enterprises had to contract their sales and purchases with home suppliers. Virtually only sales to private households and individuals were left to the vagaries of uncontrolled demand.

However, in terms of final use in current prices the consumer demand became more than a half of national income, a fact which the planners had to cope with carefully. They had, in the turnover tax, a very efficient tool which could be substituted for some important effects of the market. Differentiated rates of turnover tax enabled them to increase the final consumer price of any deficient goods to the level of the supposed market equilibrium, taking advantage especially of the price elasticity

[1] CS *Statistical Yearbooks*, basic indicators, prices indices; 25 let, pp. 106 ff.
[2] The total of transactions is computed as a sum of intermediate consumption, fixed capital investment, retail trade turnover, government purchase of goods and material services and foreign trade turnover.

of demand. With regard to this and with respect to the inflation-ary rather than deflationary gap within the economy in general, planners were not so much concerned with providing the con-sumer market with an appropriate variety of goods.[1] Thus consumer free choice had been limited to the alternatives of the centrally planned assortment. In order to obtain scarce goods, the list of which varied over time, the consumer had to spend a long time in queues or in running from one shop to another, or even had to bribe the people in the shop.

In order to master the consumer market also from the side of consumer demand, there was a steady pressure to keep the increase of incomes behind the increase of productivity. The sum of wages (wage fund), being a specific planned target for every factory and institution, provided a limit for the wage increase. The wage fund for the whole economy was to be kept in proper relation to the supply of consumer goods. This might well be calculated ex ante and in aggregate values, but the practical implementation depended on the subtlety and alert-ness with which the planning apparat was able to supply the individual goods and/or adapt the prices according to the changes in consumer demand.

Thus, although kept under the global control of the wage fund and being largely stable because of the fairly traditional consumer pattern, consumer demand nevertheless underwent certain fluctuations due to psychological rather than any other causes. The consumer became highly sensitive to indications of impending scarcity of any goods or to rumours of possible changes in prices or of a possible new monetary reform. On such occasions a purchasing boom managed to upset the pre-carious balance and planners had to cope with these by making additional adaptations in their plans or by taking emergency measures.

Another difficulty arose from the fact that the consumer, in spite of prevailing sellers' market conditions, was not always ready to buy goods of a certain type in the quantity supposed by

[1] Although the necessity to make decisions on the production of consumer goods on the basis of consumer market research had been largely acknow-ledged, any decision made on the basis of such findings had to pass through central authorities. This was a lengthy procedure, often providing the consumer with only a fragment of his wishes.

the planners, especially if these goods were too expensive and of too low quality. It happened that whereas some goods were in short supply, other goods accumulated on the shelves. This was a clear indication that the production supply did not correspond with the consumer demand.

The imbalance was not confined only to private consumption; it permeated the whole of the economy. Thus on the one hand there were always some bottlenecks, on the other, inventories accumulated in excess of the supposedly healthy ratio to the volume of production. Production costs of these goods could not be recovered from sales and constituted an additional drain on credit and therefore an additional source of inflationary pressure.[1]

Neither the planners' balancing method nor the contracting intended to commercialise, in a formal way, the planners' commands proved to be adequate substitutes for a genuine market.

(B) ACHIEVEMENTS AND FAILURES OF THE COMMAND ECONOMY

Despite all these inconsistencies and seeds of disproportion the Czechoslovak command economy achieved a considerable rate of growth. Because the planned targets were set very high (especially in industry, where the stress was laid on the means of production) and because the main duty of the working population was to fulfil the planned targets (earnings and promotion were made dependent on it) it was little wonder, in a comparatively well-developed economy with a production capacity not fully used, that production started to increase at a fast pace. Even if the official indicators, especially those reflecting gross values, imply a considerable upward bias and

[1] We have to bear in mind that in a command economy (with an efficient price control) inflationary pressure, i.e. the excess of money supply over the supply of goods and services, finds other outlets than is the direct price increase. As this pressure operates in enterprise rather than household sector, it contributes mainly to the increase of unfinished production (work in progress), to the emergence of bottlenecks and to the diversion of services from the household to the enterprise sector where the reported work can be more inflated.

often also inconsistency,[1] there is enough evidence of a truly fast pace of growth. This has been corroborated by several critical recalculations of the production and income indices as can be seen from Table 50.

Table 50

COMPARATIVE INDICES OF ECONOMIC GROWTH IN
CZECHOSLOVAKIA
$(1948 = 100)$

		1957	*1958*	*1959*	*1962*	*1965*	*1966*
1	Official index of Social Product (sum of gross values of material production) in constant prices	210	227	244	294	319	342
2	Official index of National Income (sum of net values of material production) in constant prices	202	218	232	272	277	302
3	Michal's G.N.P. index in constant prices*	179	—	—	—	—	—
4	Pešek's G.N.P. index in constant prices†	163·5	177	—	—	—	—
5	Lazarcik's G.N.P. index in constant prices‡	151	163	170	192	206	—
6	My G.N.P. index in constant prices[1]	—	—	—	—	—	279

* J. M. Michal, *Central Planning in Czechoslovakia* (Stanford, 1960) p. 231.
† Boris, P. Pešek, *GNP of Czechoslovakia in Monetary and Real Terms, 1946–1958* (Chicago, 1965) p. 44.
‡ Gregor Lazarcik, 'Czechoslovakia's GNP by Sector of Origin and by Final Use, 1937 and 1948–1965', in *Research Project on National Income in East Central Europe*, ed. by Thad P. Alton (Columbia University, 1969) p. 11.
[1] J. Krejčí, 'Vývoj ČS hospodářství v globální analýze', in *Politická ekonomie* (1968) p. 594.

---

[1] This is especially the case with the official index of industrial production and the index of industrial production computed from the social product by industrial origin in constant prices. These indices should show no substantial differences; however in 1966 the discrepancy between them was 34·5 per cent (with 1948 = 100).

Table 50 (continued)

		1957	1958	1959	1962	1965	1966
7	Official index of industrial production	270	300	333	430	480	515
8	Gross industrial production in the official social product in constant prices	218	239	257	327	361	383
9	Net industrial production in the official national income in constant prices	201	220	238	303	316	337
10	Staller's value-added index of output of industry[2]	199·5	220	242	—	—	—
11	Zauberman's index of industrial production[3]	—	—	—	295	—	—
12	Official index of personal consumption (material concept) in constant prices	172	174	183	212	232	245
13	Holešovský's index of personal consumption (comprehensive concept) in constant prices[4]	145	149	152	164	175	—
14	My index of personal consumption (comprehensive concept) in constant prices[5]	—	—	—	—	—	207

Sources: Official indices, CS *Statistical Yearbooks*.

[2] George John Staller, 'CS Industrial Growth: 1948–1959', in *American Economic Review* (1962) p. 389 (rounded figures).

[3] Václav Holešovský-Gregor Lazarcik, 'Personal Consumption index 1937 and 1948–1965', in *Occasional Papers of the Research Project on National Income in East Central Europe*, ed. Thad P. Alton (Columbia University, 1968) p. 33.

[4] Alfred Zauberman, *Industrial Progress in Poland, Czechoslovakia and East Germany, 1937–1962* (Oxford, 1964) p. 120; figure quoted here is the average of Zauberman's two alternative computations (289 and 301).

[5] J. Krejčí, loc. cit. (n. 1, p. 165 above).

These figures indicate that the upward bias of gross values is somewhere between one-fifth and one-third of the realistic evaluation, whereas the indices of net values may reflect the true development. The upward bias in the official national income index in comparison with private estimates of G.N.P.

and the differences in personal consumption indices are most probably due to the omission, in the official series, of services, the volume of which as a whole grew more slowly during the fifties than that of material production.

Nevertheless the growth of the value of goods and services represented by the G.N.P. and the growth of net industrial production and personal consumption were quite substantial. This can be stated despite two periods of setback revealed by other indicators: the first one in 1953–4 and affecting primarily investment, the second one ten years later affecting material production as a whole rather than the supply of services. These setbacks, however, bore witness to the fact that the centrally planned economy cannot get rid of fluctuations, or 'quasi cycles' as this was labelled by those Czech economists who realised the basic difficulties of the centrally planned economic system.[1]

Most disturbing, however, was that the probably unprecedented rate of growth was invalidated by two special circumstances. First that it was, within the world context of the fifties and sixties, not exceptional; many countries, even those on a high level of economic maturity such as the Federal Republic of Germany, Austria and Denmark, succeeded in reaching a faster rate of general growth than Czechoslovakia (see Table 51). In the growth of real wages Czechoslovakia has been overtaken by still more countries (ibid.). Although all these figures have only an approximate value the order of their magnitude can hardly be misleading.

Second, the conspicuous growth of material production, with heavy industry duly in the lead, had no meaning for the population unless they could participate in it to an adequate extent. Even if the relevant statistical data were withheld from the public throughout the greater part of the fifties, the working population could not be blind to the disparity between the

---

[1] Josef Goldmann–Karel Kouba, *Hospodářský růst d ČSSR*, 2nd ed. (Prague, 1969), especially pp. 46–8. The authors are well aware of the basic differences between these quasi cycles, which they could observe not only in Czechoslovak but also in Polish and Hungarian development, on one side and a free market 'capitalist' economy on the other. Whereas in the latter they result from spontaneous forces within the free market, in the former (centrally planned 'socialist' economy) they result from the miscalculation of the planning authorities.

Table 51

ECONOMIC GROWTH IN SOME ADVANCED EUROPEAN
COUNTRIES
$(1948 = 100)$

	Per capita real G.N.P. *(1966)*	Real wages *(1967)*
Federal Republic of Germany	287	213*
Austria	283	172†
Denmark	250	192
Czechoslovakia	242	157
France	199	181
Finland	194	157
Netherlands	184	193
Norway	179	165
Sweden	175	209
United Kingdom	155	153

* 1951 = 100
† 1953 = 100

Sources: Real G.N.P., UN *Yearbooks of National Income Statistics; Österreichs Volkseinkommen 1913–1963; Annual Abstract of Statistics;* J. Krejči in *Politicka ekonomie,* XVII (1969) p. 839; UN *Demographic Yearbooks.*

Real wages, all countries except Czechoslovakia: *Year Book of Labour Statistics* (1968) (International Labour Office, Geneva) p. 29; Czechoslovakia: 25 let, p. 222; *Two Year Plan Report (Průběh plnění,* pp. 316–17, 364–5).

labour input and the labour reward. Later published data summarised in Table 52–5 made it possible to get an appreciation of the magnitude of this disparity.

In the period between the Communist take-over in 1948 and the second monetary reform in 1953, per capita real national income (conceived as material product at market value)[1] increased by 50 per cent, whereas the average real wage

[1] National income in this allegedly Marxist concept is the sum of value added in mining, manufacturing, construction, agriculture, forestry, commerce, catering and in freight transport and communications insofar as they serve these industries. Expenditure on other services such as rent, interest, fees, etc., are included in the value added of industries using these services.

decreased by about 10 per cent.[1] Because of more working persons per family (as a result of mobilisation of labour force – especially women for production) the private (personal) per capita consumption of goods did not suffer the terrible setback of real wages. According to the recent official sources it was in 1953 15 per cent higher than in 1948; checked however, against earlier sources (where data for 1948 are given with more documentation and thus evoking more confidence), there was most probably only a slight increase of per capita personal consumption in that period; this is more consistent with the wage data quoted above.[2] This increase would be, however, still more questionable if services also were included to their full extent in the personal consumption index.[3]

During the following five years (1953–8) the per capita real national income increased by 33·3 per cent and the real average wage by 31·6 per cent; the per capita personal consumption of goods increased by 39 per cent. The growing employment per family brought to the population certain benefits. The real wages, however, could only in 1955–6 regain the prewar level without closing the gap between labour input and reward, a gap which originated during the first five-year plan. (Planners, by the way, considered this plan as the most successful.)

In the following three years, i.e. 1958–61, the per capita national income and real wages continued to grow on an equal basis. They increased by 20 per cent, but the per capita private consumption of goods increased by only 16 per cent.

The labour reserve, represented especially by women and by Slovak countryfolk, seemed to have been largely exhausted by the end of the fifties. Further growth could be ensured only by intensification of productivity. However, this did not happen despite the continuous increase of fixed capital. Instead, between

[1] The explicit statement on this staggering contradiction is omitted in all CS *Statistical Yearbooks* and other official publications. However, it results clearly from chaining the data of the *Two-Year Plan Report* and of *Statistical Bulletins* of 1949 and 1950 with those of the subsequent Statistical Yearbooks.

[2] The overstatement of the official data is due, apparently, to the arbitrary recalculation of 1948 national income in terms of post monetary reform (1 June 1953) prices.

[3] The official index of personal consumption comprises only material goods and a few 'material' services such as electricity and gas supply and some repair and maintenance.

1961 and 1962 the rate of growth slowed down appreciably. Then there was a slight decline and eventually stagnation until 1965, when again the per capita real income started to increase.

But what looked like disaster for the planners was not so bad for the people. In the last very bad year from the planners' point of view (1964) the per capita real national income was 2·1 per cent below the 1961 level, whereas the average real wage was 1·2 per cent higher and the per capita real personal consumption of goods 4·5 per cent higher. Per capita personal expenditure on services, the aggregate volume of which can be ascertained from data published only since 1960, increased in the same period, computed in constant prices, by 10·8 per cent.[1] Also the supply of new apartments improved in the early sixties; the increase of new flats per 1,000 population was 5·2 a year against 3·6 a year in the preceding supposedly more prosperous decade. The situation was eased also in some important non-economic respects: from 1964 there was a conspicuous opening for travelling abroad,[2] and the rate of judiciary repression of political non-conformists attained its lowest point in that year.[3]

Nevertheless the self-confidence of the planners was shattered and the reformers who had already, from the middle fifties, tried to improve the rigid system acquired a new argument. Their effort became still more substantiated as all measures so far undertaken were superficial, and when the production again began to increase the old disproportions and leakages re-appeared, as can be seen from Table 52.

Looking at the development in terms of Marx's reproduction scheme we get a particularly interesting picture of the primary distribution of the value produced by 'live labour' (value added). We discover that on the basis of official statistics (see

[1] Money epexnditure on services from the structure of personal income and expenditure deflated by the corresponding item of the cost of living index.

[2] As shown in Table 48, the number of exit permits per 1,000 population increased from 47·1 in 1963 to 147·9 in 1964.

[3] As shown in Table 47, the number of persons sentenced because of their 'anti-state' activity (Chapter I of the Penal Code) declined from 14·9 per 10,000 population of productive age in 1953 to 3·7 in 1961 and to 1·1 in 1964. Then again this ratio increased to 3·4 (1966) and declined to another lowest point – 1·2 in 1968.

Table 52

PRIMARY DIVISION OF NATIONAL INCOME
(MATERIAL CONCEPT)
IN PERCENTAGE OF THE TOTAL

	Share of individuals	Hereof individually appropriated surplus value in private sector	Share of society (surplus value at the disposal of the socialist) sector	Total surplus value (second plus third column)
1948	66·6	8·3	33·4	41·7
1949	56·1	2·5	43·9	46·4
1950	54·3	2·0	45·7	47·7
1951	48·2	1·5	51·8	53·3
1952	44·0	1·0	56·0	57·0
1953	45·5	0·5	54·5	55·0
1954	52·0	0·5	48·0	48·5
1955	52·3	0·5	47·7	48·2
1956	55·5	0·5	44·5	45·0
1957	53·8	0·5	46·2	46·7
1958	51·1	—	48·9	48·9
1959	51·4	—	48·6	48·6
1960	51·6	—	48·4	48·4
1961	50·5	—	49·5	49·5
1962	49·4	—	50·6	50·6
1963	50·9	—	49·1	49·1
1964	54·5	—	45·5	45·5
1965	55·2	—	44·8	44·8
1966	53·4	—	46·6	46·6

Sources: First and third columns, CS *Statistical Yearbook* (1968) p. 133.
Second column, estimate on the basis of ownership structure.

Table 52), which imply the Soviet interpretation of Marx's concept of value, the rate of surplus value to the variable capital increased sharply during the first five-year plan, from 0·71 in 1948 to 1·22 in 1953, then gradually declined to 0·98 in 1961 and in 1966 when the 'crisis' was overcome attained 0·87.

It might be of course objected (*a*) in general that the primary division of national income does not reveal the whole truth and that the whole process of redistribution has to be taken into account (which is certainly true) and (*b*), in particular, that in a socialist society such as Czechoslovakia private ownership of the means of production does no longer exist, and accordingly there is no scope for exploitation; virtually all, managers and producers alike, are genuine working people, the surplus value is allegedly appropriated by the whole society and to its benefit, and thus acquires another meaning.

What then happened to the increased amount of surplus value? Let us look at the final effects of the redistribution of income and let us analyse the structure of national income by type of final use. The earliest official data (disclosed in the *Statistical Yearbook* of 1966) indicated a staggering disproportion in development of the three main components of national income by use. Expressed in constant prices, aggregate personal consumption increased from 1948 to 1953 by 19 per cent, government consumption by 113 per cent and 'accumulation' by 245 per cent. Further official sources indicate the final use of the 'produced' national income in a way which is summarised in Table 53. From these data we may conclude that in 1956–70 the annual average of final distribution of national income in current prices was as follows: personal consumption 61·9 per cent, government consumption 18·1 per cent, additions to the fixed capital 11·3 per cent and other items 8·7 per cent.[1]

We have to bear in mind however that during the period concerned, consumer prices were – as a result of the well-known policy of financing industrial expansion – much higher than the wholesale prices in comparison with 1948 and before. Consumer prices were kept, by means of a turnover tax, considerably higher than production and distribution cost (labour value in Marxian terms). As investment, stocks, export and government consumption were, as a rule, paid for in wholesale prices, to which no turnover tax was added, the actual cost (labour value) ratio of personal consumption must have been correspondingly lower than computed in current prices. The magnitude of this disparity can be calculated from the difference between the aggregate expenditure structure of social product in current and constant prices (Table 54). The implicit price indices computed in this way indicate that from 1948 to 1953 retail prices in-

---

[1] Official sources indicate the corresponding shares calculated from a somewhat lesser national income total, i.e. excluding the trade balance and losses. These items form a substantial part of our residual item.

(PERCENTAGE STRUCTURE IN CURRENT PRICES)

Year	Personal consumption	Social (government) consumption	Accumulation	Of which			Difference between 'produced' and 'used' national income	
				Additions to fixed capital investment	Non-completed capital investment (work in progress)	Additions to stocks	External trade balance	Losses
1948	60·6	16·3	19·8	·	·	·	3·3	
1949	59·9	14·9	21·6	·	·	·	3·6	
1950	65·4	15·0	16·4	·	·	·	3·2	
1951	62·1	14·8	21·9	·	·	·	1·2	
1952	59·4	17·3	21·6	·	·	·	1·7	
1953	55·3	18·5	24·5	·	·	·	1·7	
1954	61·3	21·1	16·1	·	·	·	1·5	
1955	60·5	18·4	19·2	·	·	·	1·9	
1956	65·4	19·3	12·4	7·8	2·3	2·3	2·9	
1957	65·6	18·4	15·1	11·6	2·8	0·7	0·9	
1958	62·7	17·5	17·3	9·9	4·4	3·0	2·5	
1959	62·3	17·5	17·6	14·3	2·6	0·7	2·6	1·6
1960	62·7	17·3	17·1	11·3	3·2	2·6	1·3	1·1
1961	60·7	17·7	20·2	11·7	3·1	5·4	0·3	1·0
1962	61·7	18·1	18·2	9·6	2·8	5·8	1·0	1·8
1963	63·9	19·0	13·0	8·5	0·4	4·1	2·3	1·6
1964	67·1	19·9	10·1	11·6	−2·4	0·9	1·3	
1965	68·7	20·2	8·8	8·4	0·5	−0·1	0·2	2·1
1966	63·9	17·3	15·1	10·0	1·0	4·1	1·0	2·7
1967	56·3	18·1	21·7	13·2	3·5	5·0	2·3	1·6
1968	57·5	17·9	22·5	12·9	4·9	4·7	0·6	1·5
1969	56·1	16·8	24·2	12·8	6·5	4·9	1·3	1·6
1970	53·6	16·8	25·9	16·0	3·8	6·1	2·0	1·7

Source: CS *Statistical Yearbook*. Breakdown of accumulation in 1956–9; Goldmann and Kouba, *Hospodářský růst*, p. 68.

Table 54

IMPLICIT PRICE INDICES OF SOCIAL PRODUCT BY TYPE OF USE
(1948 = 100)

	1953	1955	1960	1966	1967
1 Personal consumption (= retail prices)	166·5	153·7	142·2	142·5	145·2
2 Intermediate consumption	119·5	119·9	122·9	124·3	154·7
3 Social (= government) consumption	116·2	117·7	115·4	104·4	120·4
4 Accumulation (net domestic investment)	78·5	64·8	37·1	39·7	60·7
5 Weighted (aggregate) average of lines 2 + 3 + 4 (= wholesale prices)	117·1	112·8	106·7	107·3	135·4
6 Retail/wholesale price ratio (line 1 : line 5)	142·2	136·3	133·3	132·8	107·2

Indices computed on the basis of comparison of the respective aggregates in current and constant prices in the CS *Statistical Yearbooks*.

creased to 42 per cent more than wholesale prices, whereas thereafter the difference gradually decreased to almost 33 per cent in 1966. This disparity was almost abolished by 1 January 1967, when wholesale prices were, in average, put up by 30 per cent, whereas retail prices went up by only 1·5 per cent. From this it might be inferred that 'society's' costs of (prices paid for) goods were in the period from 1949 to 1966 kept at about a third or a quarter lower than 'the population's' costs.

When we recalculate the 'produced' national income and personal consumption in 1948 prices (see Table 55) we realise

Table 55

PERSONAL CONSUMPTION IN PER CENT OF
NATIONAL INCOME (MATERIAL CONCEPT)

Year	Current prices	1948 prices
1948	60·6	60·6
1949	59·9	56·8
1950	65·4	60·1
1951	62·1	55·4
1952	59·4	51·2
1953	55·3	46·3
1954	61·3	50·9
1955	60·5	49·9
1956	65·4	51·2
1957	65·6	51·8
1958	62·7	48·4
1959	62·3	47·8
1960	62·7	48·4
1961	60·7	46·9
1962	61·7	47·4
1963	63·9	48·9
1964	67·1	50·2
1965	68·7	50·9
1966	63·9	49·1
1967	56·3	48·2
1968	57·5	49·4
1969	56·1	49·5
1970	53·6	47·3

Sources: Current prices, CS *Statistical Yearbooks*; 1948 prices, computed from the series in constant prices with the different year bases in CS *Statistical Yearbooks*.

that the personal consumption ratio dropped from 60·6 per cent in 1948 to 46·3 per cent in 1953 and since then only rarely exceeded the 50 per cent mark. This ratio reminds us of the war-time national expenditure pattern.

To complete the picture in 1948 prices, all other items of national expenditure have to be increased accordingly; in the absence of reliable price indices for individual items, however, the other half of national income can be divided among them only approximately:[1] about one-fifth of national income fell to the government consumption; another fifth to the addition to fixed capital stock; and about one-tenth to all the other items.

This tenth, which we might call summarily 'neutralised product', consists (as shown in Table 53) first of direct losses; second of the continuously active trade balance with countries abroad reflecting the steady drain on Czechoslovakia's resources to the benefit of her allies;[2] third, it consists of chronic increases in stocks resulting from disproportions between supply and demand;[3] fourth, there is also a continuous increase of the non-completed investment due especially to the continuous practice of putting the investment targets beyond the construction capacity. With respect to what has been said earlier this 10 per cent of national income represents about 20 per cent of surplus value.

This neutralised product, however, reflects only the visible

[1] Implicit price indices for individual aggregates cannot be used for the statistical deflation in this case. Accumulation into fixed capital covers, in the official statistics, an unrealistically low proportion of gross capital investment (which in its turn also is not comprehensive enough leaving out a substantial amount of construction output) and the implicit price index of accumulation as a whole (i.e. including additions to stocks – line 4, Table 54) is also hardly credible. It is therefore better to assume the general validity of our wholesale price index (line 5, Table 54) for all the other items than personal consumption. This procedure also seems to be corroborated by scattered data quoted in Čestmír Kožušník, *Problémy teorie hodnoty a ceny za socialismu* (Prague, 1964), especially pp. 94, 139 and 140.

[2] Taking into account the trade balance only (the balance of payment is not being published in sufficient detail) the net foreign investment in socialist countries totalled from 1960 to 1967 5·7 billion Kčs and in developing countries 2·8 billion Kčs, on the other hand in developed capitalist countries there was disinvestment amounting to 1·8 billion Kčs.

[3] Unsaleable goods on one side and excessive stocks of scarce goods (hoardings) on the other.

part of the economic inefficiency. Losses resulting from external trade, especially from buying expensive raw materials and selling cheap finished products, wastage connected with the huge dubious investment in extraction of poor grade minerals and industry built on the manufacturing of them, and last but not least the upkeep of a highly inflated apparat as a means of compulsion and surveillance, are too well concealed in the aggregated data to be sorted out separately.

Indirect indicators however may reveal the approximate magnitude of these sources of inefficient use of national product. The aggregate comparison of the world and domestic prices[1] of industrial goods (which form about 90 per cent of total CS export) reveal that the Czechoslovak prices were, after the inflationary move of 1948–53 and after the revaluation of Kčs in 1953,[2] about 50–60 per cent higher than world prices in which export had to be realised. This discrepancy had a tendency to increase and in the early sixties attained 100 per cent.[3] Of course these losses as far as they ensue from revaluation may be offset by cheaper imports.[4] Making allowances for this we may

[1] Domestic prices excluding turnover tax, which is not charged on export goods.

[2] It is a significant feature of centrally planned socialist economies bearing witness to the complete abolition of market conditions that an inflationary development may result in revaluation instead of devaluation of currency. Czechoslovakia was not the only example of this kind.

[3] Calculations performed by Goldmann, Kouba and Pleva in Goldmann & Kouba, *Hospodářský růst v ČSSR*, p. 83. In analysing these data, which are of course only approximate, the authors state that this disparity was due to the individual factors in the following proportions: increase of wholesale prices from 1948 to 1953, 20 per cent; revaluation in 1953, 39 per cent; increase in domestic costs from 1955 to 1963, 19 per cent (ibid. pp. 82–5).

There is also another indication of the magnitude of these losses, i.e. with respect to machinery, which from the middle fifties accounted for almost a half of export value. As the same authors mention (p. 85), calculations of the price obtained for an average kilogram of machinery exported indicated that Czechoslovakia received less than two-thirds of what advanced Western European countries received for the same quantity of material.

Finally, the incomplete data on the so-called reproduction price of foreign exchange (i.e. the Kčs equivalents of prices in foreign currencies) for the first half of 1968 indicate that one U.S. dollar was worth 31·32 Kčs and one rouble 18·32 Kčs; that is, 4·35 or 2·29 as much as the official exchange rates respectively (*Ekonomický časopis*, XVIII (1970) p. 692).

[4] It is difficult to estimate how far the parallel revaluation of currencies of other Communist countries had a countervailing effect on this offset,

evaluate the loss from the peculiar price-cost-exchange rate structure of Czechoslovak export at about 3–6 per cent of yearly national income.

The approximate effect of inefficient investment can be best demonstrated in one particular example. The fixed capital assets (in constant prices) per worker in non-ferrous metallurgy increased from 1948 to 1960 by 152 per cent, whereas in industry as a whole this ratio increased only by 22 per cent.[1] On the other hand the aggregate index of gross industrial production as a whole increased in the same period by 272 per cent, but that of non-ferrous metallurgy by only 185 per cent.[2]

There was also a considerable amount of dubious investment in other heavy industries, such as especially the construction of a huge iron and steel combinate in the Košice region in Eastern Slovakia, where both ore and fuel had to be brought from a long distance; the atomic electricity work in Jaselské Bohunice; nitrogen plant in Šal'a, etc. It is however hardly possible to assess the magnitude of these miscalculations.

Concerning the last possible source of economically ineffective resources, i.e. the excessive increase of the repressive apparat, we can only compare the military and security expenditure as reported by the state budget with corresponding items before the war. Whereas the prewar expenditure on army and police did not exceed, as a rule, 2 per cent of the gross national product (only in the period of intensive preparation for defence, in 1937, did they attain slightly more than 3 per cent),[3] in the sixties

---

because the prices among the Communist countries also are as a rule fixed according to the world price level, however, with a large scope for individual agreement.

[1] Unfortunately it is not possible to evaluate in a similar way losses resulting from the weaker bargaining position in dealing with Soviet Russia which might be of tangible magnitude especially in the early fifties.

[2] Source, CS *Statistical Yearbooks*. Unfortunately only highly inflated official indices of industrial production are available for individual industries. Indices computed on the basis of value added may reduce the difference between a general and a particular index of semi-products. Nevertheless, the difference in the production of growth is large enough, especially in comparison with the inverse ratio of investment, to give sufficient proof of the immensely low marginal efficiency of fixed capital in non-ferrous metallurgy.

[3] Jaroslav Krejčí, 'Vývoj Československého hospodářství v letech 1926–1937', in *Politická ekonomie*, XVI (1968) p. 1046. Security expenditure are added according to the prewar Statistical Yearbooks.

the corresponding expenditure was continuously between 5 and 6 per cent of the material national income, i.e. around 4–5 per cent of G.N.P.[1] This, however, does not tell the whole story.

Summing up these less easily identifiable sources of neutralisation of national production we may put them tentatively at about another 10 per cent of national income. Thus we arrive at the annual average ratio of product neutralisation to the tune of about 20 per cent of national income (net product) or 40 per cent of surplus value. It is worth while noting that 20 per cent of ineffectively utilised product corresponds to or even surpasses the average unutilised capacity during the business cycle in a free market capitalist economy such as was in operation before World War I.

It is understandable that such a disparity between labour input and output utilisation could not be concealed for long from the population involved. Every worker and every employee in production must have realised that there was something wrong with the handling of surplus value, or, to put it in more tangible terms, with the redistribution of national income and with its final use.

For those who had some understanding of economic relationships it must have been clear that the centrally planned system had been either devised in order to extort from the working population a higher surplus value (they might have realised that the high rate of surplus value was providing ample opportunity to finance both the growing needs of internal politico-economic reconstruction and simultaneously to meet international commitments going beyond the normal, mutually beneficial channels of external trade and borrowing), or that it was simply not capable of assuring an effective use of national resources.

(c) QUEST FOR A MORE EFFICIENT SYSTEM

It is understandable that the existence of disproportions and leakages reviewed in the preceding chapter must have been

[1] According to my computation of CS G.N.P. in *Soviet Studies*, XXII (1971) p. 373. It is also worth noting that prewar Czechoslovakia had a boundary of which only 4·9 per cent was covered by an allied power (Rumania). The frontier with Nazi Germany amounted to 37·4 per cent of the total frontier length. Since 1955 Czechoslovakia has had her boundary covered by 76·8 per cent of allied powers (East Germany, Poland, Hungary and U.S.S.R.).

known to those who worked in the economy and planning. It was, however, most difficult (a) to get an accurate picture of these disproportions and (b) to voice clearly opinion about them.

Concerning the difficulty of a correct picture, it has to be borne in mind that most relevant macro-economic data were kept secret until the early sixties, when only and gradually they became accessible to a wider public and thus also to all concerned. There were also different degrees of secrecy. Only men at the top could know all the data, but they had, as a rule, neither time nor qualifications to utilise them. The best qualified people had often the least access to relevant data.

Opinion not sufficiently based on quantitative analysis was of course not impressive enough, and any criticism was easily dismissed as either a professional or, more dangerously, political aberration with unpleasant consequences for the critic.

Nevertheless there were enough officials within the economic management and especially in the research institutes who were aware of the inefficiency of the system, of its rigidity and 'overdetermination' by indicators, the mutual spontaneous interconnection of reality behind which was more often than not overlooked by the planners.

The first 'reform move' was directed towards reducing the number of indicators and decentralising decision making. In the bitter-sweet atmosphere which spread throughout Czechoslovakia power élite after the Twentieth Congress of the Soviet Communist Party these ideas were incorporated into the resolution of the General Communist Party Conference on 15 June 1956. Thirty pages of its minutes are devoted to this particular topic. Shifts in decision making from central to lower organs, from government to the ministries, from ministries to enterprises or regional councils are postulated in unambiguous language. Further on, the number of centrally planned indicators had to be reduced by one-fifth and administrative work connected with the management and planning of the economy was to be simplified.[1] Not much however, happened in reality. The administrative machinery put into operation five to eight years earlier had become so strongly established and the persons

[1] Resolution of the General Conference of the Communist Party of Czechoslovakia, in *Od X. do XI. sjezdu KSČ, Usnesení a dokumenty ÚV KSČ* (Prague, 1958) p. 304 and ff.

in top positions so well accommodated that they had no interest in a change. Thus the conference resolution remained a dead letter.

Another attempt to shift the decision making from the top to lower organs and to rationalise the system of indicators, especially to lay much more stress on qualitative aspects of production, was undertaken two years later. Beginning with 1959, enterprises were allowed to accumulate funds from participation in increased profits and in depreciation allowances, and also some half-hearted steps were taken to give greater material incentives to employees for greater contribution to production.

All this modest reform however only put additional strains on the already strained relationship between the monetary and real processes within the economy. Retained profits in enterprises bolstered the amount of investment and continuous increase of wages stimulated effective consumer demand. This in juxtaposition with the labour reserve, which about that time had become exhausted, could not but produce new inflationary pressure and slow down investment in progress and eventually also production. In about three years' time the 'reform' had to be withdrawn. Only the greater stress on agricultural production, put forward according to the Soviet example, brought gradually and slowly some conspicuous results. Higher purchasing prices, higher investment and better supply of fertilisers bolstered both agricultural production and the living standard of co-operative farmers (see p. 79).

On the other hand a new impetus to the opening of the horizons of economic reasoning was given by the rediscovery of Soviet economists' discussions in the early twenties, and by the writings of Polish economists such as W. Brus and M. Kalecki, the works of whom had been translated into Czech and published in the early sixties.

But this particular challenge remained limited to the theoretical circles without direct impact on the real decision makers. Similarly the Yugoslav example, which attracted large-scale sympathy, often more for its political rather than economic reasons, and also because of traditionally very friendly feelings to this particular branch of Slavonic family. Only from 1961, when the economic rate of growth expressed in official indicators decreased and in 1962 eventually stopped at all, were more people within the power élite induced to consider economic reform seriously.

These 'reform' ideas found their echo in the resolutions of the Twelfth Congress of the Communist Party in December 1962. This time however the wording was more cautious. The following changes especially were postulated: gradual introduction of continuous planning (i.e. abolition of the uncertainty before the end of the planning period);[1] reintroduction of balances with provision for reserves (i.e. abolition of the Stalinist mobilising balances setting targets beyond the resources); improvement of the system of indicators (especially abolition of the use of gross production for computation of productivity);[2] and more effective use of material and semi-products.[3] Stress was not on decentralisation but on higher efficiency, without however the explicit statement of adequate means to this aim. This was in a way an advantage because it opened the door wider to specialist discussion.

The more serious the reform attempts became, however, the more difficult implementation turned out to be. Planners and top managers well entrenched in their power positions were reluctant to co-operate in a genuine reform. The younger generation of economists, trained first in deductive reasoning on the basis of classics of Marxism–Leninism and their Soviet

[1] This reminds one of the ideas put forward by the Social Democrat draft of the first five year plan.

[2] The old, imaginary indicators based on the gross production, however, were not abolished. As an outstanding example of this category the so-called social product should be mentioned; it represents the sum of gross values of production of all branches in the material sphere of the economy. Although several prominent Soviet economists such as S. G. Strumilin did their best to demonstrate the dubious meaning of this aggregate, the magnitude of which depends primarily on the degree of industrial integration and fluctuate with its changes, all the Communist States use this indicator even for analytical purposes. They seem to do so not so much for the pragmatic reason of easy computability of that indicator on any economic unit level, but mainly out of ill-conceived respect to Marx, who once for all conceived his reproduction scheme as the sum of $C + V + M$, i.e. the gross value of material production. For Strumilin's criticism see especially his 'Chto takoye obshchestvennyi produkt', in *Statistiko-ekonomicheskie ocherki* (Moscow, 1958) pp. 159–72.

[3] *XII. sjezd KSČ-Praha 4.–8. XII. 1962* (Prague, 1963) p. 649.

interpreters works, and then, gradually from the early sixties, in theoretical econometrics though without sufficient experience with statistical data, was better qualified to design and propose new models than to test their viability in practice. The more pragmatic and open-minded people had to work out their proposals by trial and error method, which, however, was hampered by the many vested interests.

Although the theoretical discussion was conducted with an openness unknown since 1948 and therefore brought many important issues before the public it sometimes obscured rather than illuminated the real meaning of the reform. Several points, however, resulted more or less clearly from the discussion.

First, that the national economy is a living organism the management of which is possible only on the basis of a thoroughgoing knowledge of its functioning. Therefore, it is not possible to determine individual targets arbitrarily. To put it in Kalecki's words, a central planning authority after having decided the general rate of growth had already by this fact decided on the structure of the economy. The income elasticity of demand and the technical inter-industrial (input–output) relationships are factors which determine primarily the development of the economic structure within a given rate of growth.[1]

It was widely understood that the level and structure of prices also result from these relationships. Only wages and income policy in general, and this more for non-economic reasons, can be and should be directly steered by the central authority.

The second point which resulted from the discussion can be summed up as follows: even if the central planning authority were willing to respect the functioning of the economic organism and adopt their indicators 'scientifically' according to its intrinsic laws, it has not the technical means to do so. Present econometric models are not comprehensive and/or elastic enough to cover the wide range of decisions which are necessary in the economy of everyday life. Therefore the only practical way is to leave these adaptations of individual magnitudes to the spontaneous activity of economic subjects (consumers and managers of individual production units), i.e. to the market.

The revitalisation of the market however was not understood

[1] Michal Kalecki, *Outline of the Theory of the Growth of Socialist Economy* (Czech translation from Polish original, Prague, 1965) p. 150.

in the sense of a free market economy. The market ought not to become the decisive or regulating factor of economic growth, but rather a lubricant for its more efficient development. A socialist market should be a managed market, constantly surveyed and not allowed to develop either an inflationary or a deflationary gap, or to put it more squarely, not allowed to hamper the production growth nor the growth of living standard.[1]

In order that such a market might function the monopolies had to be broken, competitive conditions brought about and new methods of planning – more indirect and global – elaborated. It was widely felt that these moves had to be undertaken with a simultaneous strengthening of the socialist character of Czechoslovak society.

There was a lot of discussion of the true essence of socialism. The concept prevailing hitherto within the power élite and seeing the essence of socialism in the tightly knit monolithic society, characterised by the state ownership of the means of production, the centrally planned and managed economy, and the monopoly of the Communist Party apparat (virtually its Politburo) in supreme decision making in all fields of social life, was put in question. Workers' participation in management, and genuine people's participation in institutions which theoretically were conceived as representative organs of the people, began to be envisaged.

In 1968 the idea of workers' councils as freely elected bodies supervising the economic management was launched. Workers' councils conceived in this way had two important meanings. On one side they provided the link with the wider concept of reform which was laboriously prepared by the research workers in the field of politology (state and law studies) and which grappled with the difficult task of how to introduce some pluralism, flexibility and safeguards of civic liberties into the one-party state. On the other hand workers' councils were to help, in a politically acceptable way, to change the management, wherever its inefficiency threatened the new development.

Of course there were many shades of opinion within this

[1] For a theoretical, Marxist justification of market relationship within a socialist economy see especially Ota Šik, *Plan and Market Under Socialism* (Prague, 1967) pp. 159 and ff.

framework of reasoning, from the most radical to the most conservative, and there were many technical issues at stake, the heated discussion of which sometimes drowned the more important problems.

Thus, although often framed in vague terms, diverted by many side issues, and obscured by the rebarbative language of past dogmatism and by the imaginary indicators, the economic reform nevertheless proceeded tentatively, aiming towards a new pattern of socialist economy, a pattern in which a symbiosis of basic, more indirect, planning with a revitalised but still managed market was sought for.

This was of course a tremendous task after 15 years of command economy with monopolistic enterprises, with a sellers' market and with managers accustomed to seeing in the fulfilment of planned targets the main economic objective. Also workers accustomed to a considerable extent to a system which laid more stress on reports on work than on the work really performed. A new system of a socialist market economy had to be introduced stage by stage, using for the transitional period administrative methods, as crutches might be used by a man recovering from a stroke.

By such means the politically determined price structure entailing a complicated system of subsidies and levies was to be abolished and a truly economic calculation re-established, monopolies were to be divided up and smaller enterprises were to receive sufficient scope for self-management.

As a first practical step to pave the way for the economic calculation and for higher efficiency, the concept of value added (gross income) was introduced as a planned indicator, on the enterprise level. Within the gross income, interest in profit was enhanced and a fierce discussion on the respective merits of gross income or profit as the basis for taxation revealed how different opinions may be on seemingly uncontroversial issues. In order to enhance economising of production factors interest (or rather taxes) on fixed capital assets, on stocks, and even wages was introduced.

Then the wholesale prices, after having been thoroughly re-examined with respect to possible real production costs[1] were

---

[1] This move was labelled as a quest for a rational price formula. Several alternatives were elaborated, taking into account different combinations of

restructured by 1 January 1967. Although this price reform, being implemented as a compromise between diverging interests, did not abolish all disproportions (price subsidies were reduced by about a half only)[1] it at least closed the gap between wholesale and retail prices, which had distorted the cost structure of Czechoslovak economy.

Price control was to become gradually less rigid. Alongside the traditionally fixed prices, new categories of limited and free prices were introduced. The weight of the latter remained, however, very small.[2] Another aim was to end with the separate and non-connected levels of wholesale, retail and foreign trade prices and to bring them into a sound economic relationship.

Further steps, especially those concerning the enterprise structure where vested interests of the old management were more at stake, were only in preparation when the whole development, still in its beginnings, was interrupted by Soviet interference.

---

labour and capital cost. For details see O. Kýn, B. Sekerka, L. Hejl, 'A Model for the Planning of Prices in Socialism ', in *Socialism, Capitalism and Economic Growth, Essays Presented to Maurice Dobb*, ed. C. H. Feinstein (Cambridge, 1967).

[1] In the first year (1967) the reduction was more substantial (by 64 per cent of comparison with 1966), but then price subsidies were again more amply used. Price subsidies, however, formed only a part (in 1968 a third) of all 'non-investment' subsidies which together attained, in 1967 and 1968, 15 per cent of national income (complete data for former years are not available). This is another indication of the magnitude of the price-cost discrepancies even when economic reform was already in progress and had abolished a good deal of them. (Data from CS *Statistical Yearbooks*.)

[2] Retail prices remained mainly fixed (to about 87 per cent of turnover in 1967, the remaining 13 per cent being freed). Wholesale prices fell mainly under the limited prices category (around 80 per cent of turnover). Data from Josef Rosa, 'Theoretical and Practical Experience with the New System of Planned Management', in V. Háčik *et al. The Finance of Czechoslovakia in the New System of Management* (Bratislava, 1968) p. 7.

CHAPTER FOUR

Why Change Again?

The interplay of societal forces in postwar Czechoslovakia which eventually culminated in the 1968 events is often interpreted as an example of economic troubles or even crisis evoking the need for change and thus precipitating – within the closely interconnected and rigid system – a political crisis.

This interpretation, however, does not reveal the whole truth on this very serious attempt to develop the already established Soviet-type socialist system into a more humanitarian one with a fair degree of civic liberties and pluralistic constellation of power.

Even this presentation of the issue, the complexity of which cannot be overlooked, indicates that the Czechoslovak development can hardly be understood in terms of Marxian clichés which, paradoxically, seem to be more readily accepted at face value in the West than in the East.

Man is not only a machine for consumption, which so many relationships within modern industrial society tend to make him; he is a sensible organism reacting also to less tangible societal issues, especially in periods when strongly emotionally or morally tinged alternatives are at stake.

Something of the latter type occurred in the middle sixties in Czechoslovakia when the majority of the population, for different reasons and in different intensity, experienced growing dissent with the obstinacy of the Stalinist establishment in their country. The particularly important element in this development was the eventual participation in it of the substantial part of the ruling strata. Otherwise the dissent could not have acquired such a politically relevant magnitude and led, up to a point, to successful action.

The spread of discontent among the ruling strata was due to

three main causes which, although being differently felt by individual social groups, gradually coalesced into one general complex longing for change.

The first and most basic cause of dissent was, although it might sound absurd in a world inclined to accept a materialistic interpretation of history, a moral malaise produced by the shock of Stalinism grafted by the combined means of naïvety, fraud and force on to Czechoslovak society. It is hardly conceivable that at least some Communists in ruling positions could not have realised the moral insanity of what was happening during the early fifties, but they were afraid to voice their opinion. After the worst excesses of Stalinism had been expounded by the Soviet representatives themselves, even those who were afraid to see or did not want to see could allow their conscience, even if heavily deformed by the doctrine of hatred, to awaken.

Awakened conscience produced the need for rehabilitation first of Communists, then, reluctantly, also of other victims of prefabricated trials. This mood, however, came up against the opposition of a tiny group at the top, aware of their active participation in the persecutions of the past and therefore afraid of losing their position if the rehabilitation proceeded too far. Thus a tension was aroused within the Party. Of all its cadres it was especially the cultural intelligentsia who, being most aware of both Czech democratic tradition and Marx's original teaching, became the spokesmen for fresh outlooks and promoters of more open views than Stalinist dogmatism admitted. There was involved not only the moral issue itself but a general intellectual attitude in which open-mindedness and objectivity began to be claimed as desirable values.

However, the undisguised vanguard of the open-minded approach to all social problems was recruited from two particular groups: writers and the young intelligentsia, students. The first occasion when many writers happened to express their unorthodox views (for the time being only on literature – especially on the role of writer in socialist society) was their congress in 1956. The first articulated action of the students can be seen as the First of May celebration of 1957,[1] when spon-

---

[1] Already a year earlier students had distinguished themselves, on the occasion of the First of May parade, by ridiculing some sacred tenets of Marxist–Leninist education. This incident however did not exceed the

taneous ad hoc gatherings of students put forward demands for democratisation and liberalisation of the school system and implicitly also of society; these desiderata included also one highly explosive postulate – the abolition of Marxism–Leninism as a compulsory subject in all university curricula.

Although the spontaneous eruptions of feelings were easily suppressed (there were some arrests and some expulsions from studies) the ideas launched during those days continued to gain ground not only among the student population.[1] Departments of Marxism–Leninism which because of their sterile orthodoxy were exposed to the above-mentioned assault in 1957, seem to have taken their criticism seriously. Either because of the awakened conscience, or because of the influx of new blood (largely of workers' origin) or because of the relaxed pressure, they gradually changed their attitudes and eventually developed, during the middle sixties, into the focuses of heretic ideas, combining heterodox teaching with open windows to the outside, especially to Western influences.

At the same time the younger generation of university teachers at large and of research workers in the Academy of Sciences started to make up their own minds about the creative approach to Marxism, and thus to transform this formal slogan into reality. To anybody it must have been clear that a true creativity cannot be confined by any decisions of institutions, however authoritative. It must also have been clear that the main practical interest, the main target of this creative approach was to bring about a change in the organisation of society which would not only make an end of the Stalinist perversions of Socialism but also prevent the recurrence of its features. This was the primary aim of the open-minded and morally conscious intelligentsia within the Communist Party, an aim widely supported by the public as soon as the latter had grasped that this had become the real issue.

---

bounds of joking. Nevertheless the authorities took these events seriously and similar students' processions were forbidden during the following years.

[1] An important factor of the events was the fact that in the May demonstration, as the reports of arrested persons testify, the working youth also took a considerable part. Also in the subsequent development there was a comparatively frequent friendly intercourse between different strata of the young generation.

Another important reason for dissent within the ruling strata resulted from the particular ethnic dualism in the Czechoslovak State, which after a thorough-going homogenisation of Czechoslovak society in most other aspects remained the main dividing factor, second only to that of rulers and ruled. There is a certain self-annihilating logic in the homogenisation drive of a Soviet-type society which does not respect, in a relevant way, any other differentiation than that emanating from the hierarchical position of authority and power based on ideological and political conformity.

After World War II Czechoslovakia re-emerged as a State of two nationalities. Slovakia has obtained a good deal of autonomy which survived after the Communist take-over in 1948 although in a much attenuated form. Nevertheless it has proved useful in bringing Slovakia closer to the Czech standard both in economic and cultural aspects. However, as socialisation of the means of production coupled with a levelling incomes policy proceeded, and social homogenisation of Czechoslovak society attained its apogee, the men at the top tried to get rid also of the dualistic character of the state. The 1960 Constitution which proclaimed the Czechoslovak Republic as a Socialist one (as the second to Soviet Russia in history) at the same time reduced Slovak autonomy to some rather formal paraphernalia.[1]

This move, however, coincided with incipient relaxation of judicial and administrative repression of people suspected of possible political opposition,[2] and also with the campaign within the Party to rehabilitate those of its members who fell victims of Stalinist trials; among them, incidentally, were also Slovak representatives sentenced because of opposition to Prague centralism, an opposition qualified as bourgeois nationalistic deviation. Therefore, the virtual abolition of Slovak autonomy could not be accepted with the submissiveness to which the top leaders grew accustomed in the period of terror.

---

[1] For the development of constitutional issues of Czech-Slovak relationship see Galia Golan, *The Czechoslovak Reform Movement* (Cambridge, 1971) p. 189 and ff.

[2] In 1960, for the first time since the Communist take-over in 1948, an amnesty for political prisoners was granted, releasing about 11,000 persons from prisons and labour camps.

The third main reason for discontent, which affected also the ruling strata, originated not in the superstructure (as the above-mentioned dissensions would be labelled by Marxists) but at the very bottom of the economic basis. As shown in chapter 3 (B), the material production ceased to increase from 1961 to 1962 and in 1963 and 1964 suffered a slight decline. This produced a shock among the planners and apparatchiks, who in the continuous growth of material production saw the main target of socialist economy and also the main argument for its superiority over the capitalist way of production. As the stagnation extended for three successive years and a scapegoat could not be found among the remnants of capitalism (these were destroyed by the second monetary reform in 1953, by the subsequent collectivisation of agriculture and last but not least by judicial and administrative repression), it was clear that there was something wrong with the economy which must be put in order.

Until then dissent with the economic development was limited to those people who in some way suffered or were irritated by it. These were in the first place those who suffered expropriation, but they were a minority which gradually disappeared by the natural process of dying out.

Second, there were those whose income remained, as a result of the levelling policy, below the average growth; in this respect the new intelligentsia often experienced the same misgivings as the old, especially as they realised that in other countries, including socialist ones, their counterparts were in a better relative position.[1]

Third, the discontent was spreading among those who could not, because of the wage ceiling (laid down not only for the whole enterprise in the planned wage fund but for individuals also), earn more money in a legal way, although they were able and willing to work more.

Fourth, discontent arose among those who although earning enough, could not freely spend their higher income on things such as flats and maintenance services, cars and occasionally also more elementary goods such as meat, eggs, fruit and bedding,

---

[1] International comparison, enabled by gradually allowing people to travel abroad (partly also to the West) and to make comment in the press or other media, became an important element of the fervent during the middle sixties.

etc. The latter difficulties were apparent especially during the fifties and as a rule more felt in the countryside than in large industrial and/or administrative centres.

Fifth, there was a widespread feeling that the general level of personal income did not correspond to the labour input which was producing much more than the share which the working population received and than was reasonably utilised by society as a whole.

Although differently motivated, the misgiving was directed against the economic system, the unpopularity of which was additionally aggravated by difficult conditions of shopping. In the predominantly seller's market, the customer was more often than not in the position of a supplicant.

But all this did not shatter the confidence of those who were controlling the means of production and distribution at the top level. They regarded these defects of the command economy as temporary phenomena, caused mainly by some minor and avoidable mistakes in the planning technique rather than by the lack of market conditions.

When, however, the reported growth, which for the common man often appeared either imaginary or at least much exaggerated, stopped also in terms of the planners' indicators, as happened in the early sixties, some of the rulers realised that there might be something wrong with their rule.

We have to put into proper dimensions both the social relevance of this particular economic stagnation and its impact on the traditional way of handling economic difficulties in a Soviet-type state.

Concerning the gravity of the economic stagnation, we have to bear in mind the different apperception of reality by different groups of population. Planners and apparatchiks saw the economic reality through the prism of indicators reflecting their political interest and envisaged this particular presentation of economic reality as most important for the whole state of society. People who largely considered the economic merits or demerits of the régime according to its effects on their life in a more complex way, did not think in terms of some specific indicators, the veracity of which was anyhow widely doubted, but in terms of the balance of their respective efforts and rewards generally. An important element of the situation was also the extent to which they could break through the different administrative barriers hampering their self-assertion.

Looking at the development of the early sixties from the people's perspective the situation was not so gloomy as it appeared to be for those who were captives of their ideological and professional preoccupations. As we have already shown in chapter 3 (B), there was a lot of readjustment in the economic structure. Visible wastage was considerably reduced and consumer supply somewhat improved in housing and services. Accidentally the situation was eased also in some important non-economic aspects such as travelling abroad, judiciary repression, screening practices, etc. However among the planners there was growing concern about the future. The stagnation of material production bore witness to the fact that the traditional incentives of the planned economy provided no guarantee for the continuous growth.

Concerning the impact on the traditional way of handling economic difficulties, it has to be viewed against the background of chronic inclination to undertake non-substantial reforms whenever difficulties emerged. A steady reorganisation became a permanent feature of the Czechoslovak politico-economic system after World War II. Every time when something was going wrong the first reaction was not to look for and eventually heal the roots but to make shifts in organisation. Economic units were put together, then disconnected and again united into larger units; the methodical content of indicators was changed. New ministries and ministerial commissions were formed, then again abolished or united with others or at least re-named. Nor did the school system (especially universities) and territorial units (districts and regions) escape this chronic propensity for reorganisation. 'Delimitation' became a well-known phenomenon which periodically absorbed a good deal of time and energy of the people involved. However, all these changes affected real life only by inflicting on it an additional trouble: moving people to other jobs or places and delimitating their activities anew.

From about 1963 however change began to be envisaged as a more serious matter: not as a mere reorganisation or change in the planning technique but as a comprehensive reform; mistakes began to be grasped in their complexity, and this realisation penetrated even among the people near to the top.

Thus gradually the idea of a genuine economic reform originated. Although differently conceived in different parts of the political and economic apparat and differently understood and interpreted by management and economic experts, it nevertheless aimed tentatively towards a new pattern of socialist economy, a pattern in which basic, rather indirect, planning should be combined with a managed, not completely free market.

Of course, with respect to what we said earlier on the other reasons for discontent among the ruling strata, the reform could not aim only at change in economic relationships. As Stalinism was a complex system so its abolition could not be achieved except by concerted action in all aspects of social life. The economic reform was only one aspect of the Reform of the whole system, a Reform by which a still more difficult symbiosis had to be achieved – that of one-party leadership with a dualistic (two nation) state, and a pluralistic constellation of power; this endeavour was marked by particular stress on guaranteeing to the citizen, in a different way from in the West, those basic rights and liberties which form the core of values of the West European civilisation.

This part of the Reform falls, however, outside the scope of this particular study. Only one special feature linking political and economic aspects of the Reform, should be stressed in this context; the endeavour to establish genuine elective workers' councils and to give them a decisive voice in industrial management. That this was one of the main sins against the Soviet type of socialism has been proved by subsequent events.

On the other hand, the other special feature of the Reform – the explicit concept of Czechoslovakia as a federal, i.e. in fact dualistic, state did not apparently arouse any Soviet opposition. On the contrary, the legitimate Slovak aspiration to equal treatment was used as a pretext to oppose the validity of the Fourteenth Party Congress, which defended the national self-determination of both nations (Czechs and Slovaks alike) against a common and much more formidable challenge than could

---

[1] Its main aspects are dealt with in Vladimír V. Kusín, *The Intellectual Origins of the Prague Spring* (Cambridge, 1971) esp. pp. 97–123.

ever be produced by any Czech pressure on Slovakia. After having served this purpose, however, Slovak self-determination became less important and a renewed tendency towards a more unitary state seems to be gaining ground again, as the last and least pronounced Counter-Reform move in Czechoslovakia.

As we have said already, the leading stratum in the Reform movement was the cultural intelligentsia, which was of all the social groups most exposed to Stalinist pressure. On the one hand, if willing to collaborate, they were most cajoled and bribed, on the other hand if refraining from doing so or if somehow deviating, they were the most insecure in their jobs and personal status. No wonder that the main achievement which this group expected from the Reform was intellectual freedom.

The technical intelligentsia was interested in the change for other reasons. Although not harassed directly and enjoying a comparatively secure position, it felt frustrated by the lack of adequate compensation and of creative self-assertion within a system where everything was planned and commanded from above and the technicians had only to find means to fulfil the orders, in which they were often hampered either by the 'over-determination' of the planned indicators or by administrative vexation and secrecy of research. They expected from the Reform primarily greater efficiency, both of technical facilities and of human organisation. Greater freedom, at least with respect to contacts abroad, was seen as a prerequisite of this development.

Both these groups of intelligentsia, defined as people with higher and upper secondary education had considerably increased since the war. In 1955 they formed 8·6 per cent in 1966, 17·4 per cent of the labour force. Their growing influence however, was not only in their numbers, it resulted mainly from the peculiar features of Czechoslovak society, where social stratifications had never been rigid in modern times. The decomposition of social status had attained a fair degree even before the war and continued with an accelerated pace during the postwar period of levelling and socialisation. This process was particularly enhanced by punitive or prophylactic measures such as sending people from professional and clerical to manual jobs which unintentionally helped towards a better understanding between intelligentsia and the working class.

No wonder that both groups of intelligentsia, although

differently participating in the critique of the system and in the Reform programme, expressed their concern with those aspects of the system which the other strata of population must have felt as their own as well if they began to think of the reasons of their dissatisfaction, i.e. lack of freedom and efficiency.

The workers seemed to be least active at the beginning. Deprived of genuine representation both in trade unions and factory councils and having experienced already in the early fifties the hard hand of rulers originating from their own class, they lost interest in public affairs and concentrated on the small gains which they could achieve by exploiting the holes within the system of industrial planning and organisation. However, when they felt the changed climate on the upper floor of society and realised the opportunity for getting a fairer share in the surplus value through their self-assertion in political life and management, they participated and committed themselves in a way which surprised everybody who had lived among them years previously.

Only in some privileged and/or subsidised industries such as mines or nonferrous metallurgy, where the introduction of market conditions could have had negative effects on wages and employment, were the workers more inclined to give ear to the defenders of the status quo, who themselves were gradually losing ground even among the apparatchiks. The workers' partial misapprehension of the reform, however, widely differed from region to region and was mainly dependent on local personal contacts with the people of the Party and other apparats.

Of the social groups as a whole only the peasants, decreasing in number each year, remained rather silent during this period. Those who survived in their villages the drastic collectivisation of the fifties enjoyed their improved living standard during the early sixties. They gradually attained a material standard, if not higher, at least equal to that of industrial workers. No other social group have experienced such an advance in this period. Therefore it is little wonder that the peasantry, which is generally inclined to conservatism and which in this particular case was every year more and more made up of the older generation,[1] was not incited like the other social groups to take

[1] The proportion of people under 20 in agriculture decreased from 13·3 per cent in 1930 to 4·2 per cent in 1962.

part in the political activisation. On the other hand, when confronted with prospects for a greater vocational self-assertion they did not refrain from using these opportunities.

Thus, with the exception of a part of the ruling apparat (especially unpopular and/or unqualified people going in fear of losing their posts), supported occasionally by workers in privileged industries or enterprises, all the social groups within Czechoslovak society gradually became interested in a substantial change of its politico-economic system. What united them were not – with the exception of the call for a better use of resources – particular economic interests (these were often different and might easily have developed into contradictory ones) but the longing for a freer and more efficient society; or, as it was labelled by the man who, although more pushed than pulling, nevertheless grasped the issue and by the accidental interplay of moral, ethnic and economic forces emerged at the top, 'socialism with a human face'.

Index

ABBREVIATIONS

CS Czechoslovakia, Czechoslovak
Kčs Czechoslovak Crown
KSČ Communist Party of Czechoslovakia